Jean Pearce

More Foot-loose in Tokyo

The Curious Traveler's Guide to Shitamachi and Narita

with Makiko Yamamoto *and* Fumio Ariga
drawings by Joana Joy

New York · WEATHERHILL · *Tokyo*

First edition, 1984

Published by John Weatherhill, Inc., of New York and Tokyo, with editorial offices at 7–6–13 Roppongi, Minato-ku, Tokyo 106, Japan. Protected by copyright under terms of the International Copyright Union; all rights reserved. Printed and first published in Japan.

LCC 83–051221   ISBN 0–8348–0190–6

Contents

Foreword

ALL CITIES HAVE a *shitamachi,* a downtown, a section earlier, older, a place where history lives. Paris has its Left Bank; New York, its below-Canal-Street; London, "The City." None of these, however, makes so much of its downtown as does Tokyo of its Shitamachi. To the Japanese, particularly the Tokyoite, the capital is divided. There is Shitamachi and there is the rest.

The rest, the Yamanote, is by far the larger part of Tokyo but one hears little talk of it. Instead, it is the Shitamachi that is referred to, made much of. Here is something special; even now here are a people unique. Tokyo residents visit it as though it were a different city. Which, in a way, it is: Shitamachi and its people are heirs of modern Tokyo's past—the times of old Edo.

Someone born in New York's Fulton Street or along London's South Bank is just another city dweller, but someone born in Tokyo's Shitamachi is something else. He is (if a product of three generations in that locality) a real Edokko, a child of Edo. In himself he embodies and displays a number of premodern qualities and thinks of himself as being open, generous, hot-tempered, quick-witted, inquisitive, generous, quick to offend and quick to forgive. He is spontaneous and impulsive, both traits one does not associate with the modern Japanese.

So different does he find himself from other Tokyoites, and so different do they find him, that Japanese commentators have ventured parallels. The Edokko is the Cockney of Tokyo. Though the analogy is imprecise, there *is* a difference between the man from Shitamachi and the man from the Yamanote. He has been found unpolished, rude, self-seeking; he has also been discovered to be

7

the salt of the earth, unrepressed and self-fulfilling. Accounting for this difference are several theories.

One is that once all Japanese were like him. Then came the closure of the country, the official adaption of Confucian morality and four hundred years of the Tokugawa government's police state. This combination produced the modern Japanese, with all his faults and virtues. The men of Shitamachi, however, escaped.

The reason has to do with the lay of his land. Other cities grew up around rivers as well and hence their downtowns are associated with ports and commerce. Though Shitamachi has its river, the Sumida, it did not grow around it—nor, indeed, is Tokyo a city which naturally grew from any commercial point. It—like Washington, D.C., or Brasilia—was orginally an artificial city in that it did not accidentally burgeon. Rather, a point between the Musashino plains and the Sumida delta was appointed the proper place for a city and the castle was built. The city then grew more or less naturally around this urban implant.

If you quarter a map of Tokyo, using the Imperial Palace as center, the Shitamachi is only a small section of the northeastern sector. Though it now includes Tsukiji and Kanda, Ueno and Asakusa, the river and some of the land—Mukojima—beyond it, it originally encompassed only the land west of Ueno. It remained more or less deserted during the earliest days of Edo—therefore, Tokyo's Yamanote really predates its Shitamachi.

Early in the seventeenth century a large Buddhist temple was constructed on this plain, near the river. The northeast is in Asia the traditionally unlucky direction and the monks' duties were to purify this unhealthy place with their presence, and hence protect both Edo Castle and the town growing so rapidly around it. (The temple—or one more or less like it—is still there: the famed Asakusa Kannon.) The plain itself was regarded as unhealthy and unlucky, as well as being at the ends of the earth.

Consequently, since it was so undesirable and so distant from both the castle and bustling Nihombashi (rapidly becoming the commercial center of the country), it was deemed the location of a satellite city when the Tokugawa government decided to install a few more reforms and get rid of some of Edo's undesirables.

The luxurious teahouses, the courtesan establishments, the theaters, the brothels—all were moved northeast into Shitamachi. In addition, as Otemachi and Nihombashi became more and more official and commercial, smaller establishments catering to such specific pursuits as eating, drinking, and enjoying oneself, moved farther and farther out, closer and closer to the lively precincts of the Asakusa Kannon. Eventually this resulted in a new town, Asakusa, and just north of it the famed licensed quarter, the Yoshiwara.

This was the beginning of Shitamachi. It is also what we see when we think of old Edo—the world of actors and courtesans, woodblock prints, traditional crafts, the whole floating world of the *ukiyo-e*. This did not exist in the Yamanote—though people from uptown were the best customers for artists, artisans, and artistes of the Shitamachi. It was here that the popular arts and pleasures of the city were found and where, for centuries, they remained.

Official Japan had regulated the human appetite to a geographical position and there it left it. Though there was many an investigation, many a reform, Asakusa and its environs were never subjected to the pressures inflicted upon the rest of the capital. Though there were various politically motivated cleanups, various high-sounding promulgations, the authorities never completely closed down the pleasure-town in the northeast.

Nor did they encourage it to share in the Meiji-period Westernization of Japan and the rise in land-value prices which accompanied a resultant boom economy. Consequently it was not long before only Shitamachi held the look of old Edo with its traditional architecture and increasingly quaint ways. In rapidly changing Tokyo it was the despised Edokko who became heir to the Tokugawa tradition. It was also he who, almost untouched by four centuries of Tokugawa repression, remained impulsive, enthusiastic, direct.

This, at least, is the story. Part of it is probably true since even now the third-generation child of old Edo is in so many ways different from his uptown brother. Or perhaps, as in the Cockney tradition, generations have imitated a beau ideal and hence created it.

In any event, Shitamachi—having been allowed to go its own leisurely and old-fashioned way and thus avoid the excesses of hurried, modern Tokyo—has become the place where what little of the old the city retains is still on view, the single section where traditional ways and attitudes remain. Yamanote, earlier though parts of it are, contains no history; Shitamachi, later though it is, has it all.

Though twice destroyed (along with much of the rest of Tokyo), first during the 1923 Kanto earthquake, second during the 1945 American firebomb raids, Shitamachi has always rebuilt itself in the old pattern. Houses, single or double story, are made of wood and tile; the streets and lanes meander in their human and eccentric way; in Fukagawa one can still see the old canals of the premodern city.

Old-fashioned rice crackers are still sold singly in the shops; the futon bedding is still hung out to air in the time-honored fashion; there are many kimono stores and one still hears the nostalgic clatter of the wooden geta clogs. In addition, relics from the past are still on the street: that Meiji-period invention the *chindonya* band is still to be seen and heard, though it may now be advertising the opening of a *pachinko* (pinball) parlor. Tokyo's single great festival, the Sanja Matsuri, a fertility rite only slightly disguised, still occurs in Asakusa every spring.

In the summer there are paper lanterns and fireworks. Half the populace, it seems, is out strolling in light cotton yukata. There are caged insects, the goldfish-seller with his bowls and poles; candied squid on sticks, Meiji-era sugar drops—Shitamachi is one of the few places in the city where you can still buy that straw-colored, lemon-flavored drink, *ramune,* which comes in a green-glass bottle with a marble for a stopper. It is then, seeing this, that the romantic foreigner feels that he has truly, finally, come to Japan.

The Edokko, and the others of Shitamachi, are not unaware of their differences, nor of the fact that other Tokyo people time-travel in their district. They make the most of their anomaly, their different accent (Shitamachi is pronounced with the *i* elided: *sh'ta'-ma-chi*), their unique view of their little world.

Little and vanishing—they do well to make the most of it while they may. What the Tokugawa government, the earthquake, and war could not accomplish, peace and prosperity are bringing about. The price of land in Shitamachi is no longer lower than that of the rest of the city. In fact, it is in some places higher—as the megalopolis spreads out beyond the horizon Shitamachi is very convenient, very close to the center of things. The consequence is that high-risers are rising, the supermarkets are moving in—and whole sections of older buildings monthly disappear. Already the once picturesque banks of the Sumida are gone—taken over by concrete embankments and stilted superhighways. Soon Shitamachi will exist only as a place name, the Edokko will be scattered, and the last of old Tokyo will have vanished.

There is no saving it, but there is still time to enjoy it, this small pocket of history, this glimpse of the Japanese as they once were, this small bulwark against time, change, and necessity.

And here, in this book, are the means to enjoy it—the first English-language guide to old Tokyo, by one of those who knows and loves it best.

Jean Pearce is perhaps the single Westerner most knowledgeable about Tokyo. There may be foreign scholars who know more in depth but they do not know so much about so many things. There may be others who know about a lot of things but they do not know them the way she does—through actual experience.

Her invaluable column in the *Japan Times* has assured that she really must get up and find out. In discovering "how to get things done in Japan" (the title of her column) she has found out much else. She has discovered Tokyo as few foreigners before her have. Much of her knowledge she put into her earlier volumes, including *Foot-loose in Tokyo*. But there is always more, and she is always finding out things, and so here is the essential guide to Shitamachi, to old Tokyo.

Not only does she know about things—places, sites, stores— she also knows, equally important, about the atmosphere which makes the place so what it is. And it is this, along with all the information, which makes me treasure her book.

If to love is to understand, and there must be an old Japanese proverb that says as much, then in this book Jean Pearce has shown us the way.

DONALD RICHIE

Autumn, 1983

Directions

IT IS APPROPRIATE that a guidebook should start with directions even though these days it often seems there are far too many. Life is filled with labels to read, instructions to master, processes to learn. One longs for the simpler days of the past. And that is where we are going, back in history to discover Shitamachi.

To know where you are going it is usually necessary to define your destination. For Shitamachi, this is not necessarily true. It is hard to put a boundary to it. "The old downtown of Edo days," you could say, turning to the dictionary to translate the word: *shita* (down), *machi* (town). That, however, is not satisfactory because there was never a "downtown" as we think of it today.

"Tokyo is a complex of villages," is often said to define the present capital. How much more true that was in the days of Edo, when the shoguns ruled from their capital in the east and the emperors held court with poetry parties and incense ceremonies in Kyoto. It was even less a city then. Merchant houses, trades, and centers for entertainment formed clusters, each in its own sector.

Nor can Shitamachi be defined only in terms of Edo, because it remains very much in existence today, and many nostalgically seek out the "Shitamachi mood" or the "Shitamachi taste" in the streets of the old city.

Shitamachi is perhaps best described as a state of mind, a feeling, a point of view, and those who go in search of the past will find it wherever it exists, the small pockets that continue to resist the uniformity that all too often accompanies modernization.

Tokyo is full of such pockets, though there are those who would disagree. "Nothing remains of Edo," you will be told. "It has all been destroyed."

Not quite all. When Emperor Meiji claimed Edo for his capital in 1868 and changed its name to Tokyo, the next goal was to catch up with the West. In the process, much of old Edo disappeared. Wood construction was replaced by imposing red-brick buildings, and the city gradually took on a modern look. But the Meiji era ended too, and we are told nothing remains from those days—or, more accurately, very little. Next was Taisho, of which, of course, very little remains, the process of change having been hastened by the Great Kanto Earthquake of 1923. Our present era, Showa, has accelerated the destruction of the old as Tokyo rebuilt itself from an unprecedented disaster: the firebombings of World War II. Some (though it is rarely Japanese who make the observation) might also include as a disaster the creation of a modern industrial giant whose products spill out to overwhelm markets throughout the world. Japan has come a long way from Shitamachi.

And even so, with all that said, much remains of the past for those who would seek it out. Against modern Tokyo's chrome and concrete, it takes very little to remind one of yesterdays: perhaps a weathered wooden house, shades of brown and gray in pleasing harmony; or a narrow lane—it would seem you could extend your arms and touch the houses on either side—lined with flowers and plants growing luxuriantly in plastic buckets and tin cans, with a grandfather, baby strapped *ombu*-style on his back, coaxing them to grow properly; or perhaps your Shitamachi is to be found in festival drums and temple fairs, in paper lanterns and singing insects.

You will also find that the people of Shitamachi are somehow different from those usually met in the city, but we will leave that pleasant discovery for you to make as you have your own experiences in what remains of old Tokyo.

There is very little that can be said about Shitamachi beyond what Edward Seidensticker recounts in his outstanding book *Low*

City, High City. Shitamachi is low city, home for the common people. Yamanote is high city, where the aristocrats built their mansions.

"The Low City has always been a vaguely defined region, its precise boundaries difficult to draw," he writes. "It sometimes seems as much an idea as a geographic entity."

Then, of course, because he is a researcher as well as a scholar and author, he provides us with a workable description, but the point is clear that no matter how precise the definition, it is still hard to pencil in the boundaries. Today, for many, Shitamachi is what remains of the past, or reminds of it, whatever the date of its founding or the area in which it exists.

Each era claimed some of this past in its modernization programs. In addition, the low city was often devastated by floods and fires as it still is today. Shitamachi suffers most in times of disaster, and even now the consensus is that when (rarely is this expressed as 'if') the next earthquake comes, the greatest loss of life and property will be in Tokyo's low city.

Seidensticker contributes a touch of cheer to this gloomy outlook. He quotes a visitor who returns to Meiji Tokyo after being gone for a year or so. "Old Edo has passed away forever," the man says, observing the rapid modernization. But then Seidensticker wisely adds, "Edo has gone on passing away ever since."

If this is true, and surely it is, it is also obvious that there must always be something left to pass away. It is those places that this book seeks out. Where they are no more, you will learn what once was there, and perhaps a legend, a marker, or a temple good-luck charm will still bear testimony to the past.

I am grateful to Seidensticker for writing an introduction to *Foot-loose in Tokyo,* the companion volume to this one, which describes the stops along the Yamanote, the commuter rail line that encircles most of "high city." I am also happy to have his definitive history of Shitamachi, and even happier I did not have it sooner. If I had, I could never have written this book; I would constantly have turned to him for quotations and anecdotes.

And now, the directions. Start anywhere. Choose whatever itinerary appeals to you. Each is a complete excursion, even to the souvenirs. And the good part about your travels is this: you can always be sure of getting to where you are going, knowing what you are seeing when you are there, and being certain that you can find your way home when you have completed your explorations. Addresses and phone numbers of key places are provided in both English and Japanese in the footnotes, and characters have been inserted in the text so that as you progress along the streets of Shitamachi, you can keep your finger firmly placed in the book, there to point out where you are going if you need assistance in finding your destination. Shopkeepers and others along the way will be happy to point you off in the proper direction.

But don't wait. Get started. Because one day there may be nothing left of Shitamachi but memories.

Negishi: Foot of the Cliff

SOME ITINERARIES ARE SHORT, a leisurely stroll through a few blocks that somehow retain the past. You sense it rather than see it, and it is difficult to say precisely where the difference lies between Shitamachi and other parts of the city.

Well, for one thing, there are the rows of flowers and plants alongside narrow alleyways and filling windowsills. Then there are the people; they have a directness, an acceptance of the world around them, a natural friendliness that is not so apparent in other parts of the city. They do not seem always to be in a hurry; somehow there is more time in Shitamachi.

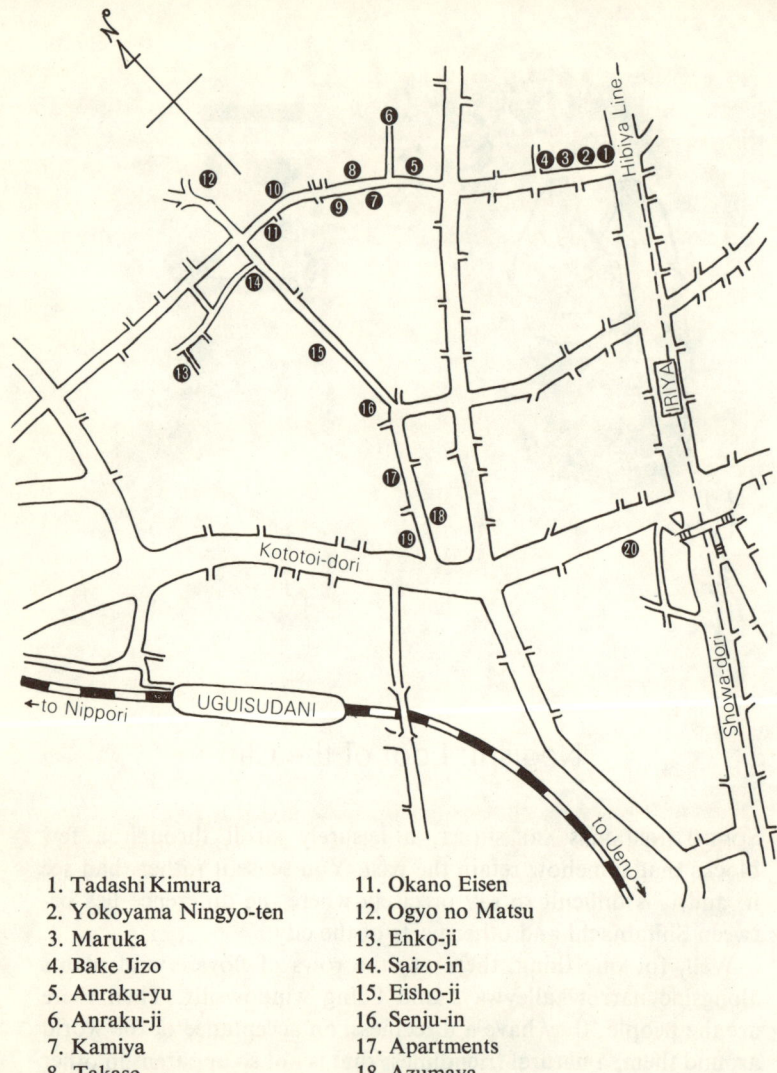

1. Tadashi Kimura
2. Yokoyama Ningyo-ten
3. Maruka
4. Bake Jizo
5. Anraku-yu
6. Anraku-ji
7. Kamiya
8. Takase
9. Komatsuya
10. Ebiya Some Kojo
11. Okano Eisen
12. Ogyo no Matsu
13. Enko-ji
14. Saizo-in
15. Eisho-ji
16. Senju-in
17. Apartments
18. Azumaya
19. Yoden-ji
20. Kishibojin

Negishi means "foot of the cliff," and once it was. On top was Ueno, in Edo days a bluff overlooking the sea. We selected Negishi as our first stop because the circular route, from subway station and back again, is easy to follow. You will see shops where traditional crafts and food products are made and, of course, sold. Excursions are more enjoyable when you can take home souvenirs. There are temples and shrines with old legends and ancient treasures. You can stop for lunch and then relax at an old-style neighborhood bath. Business continues as usual at the shops, the usual for many of them stretching back over several generations.

How long your tour will take depends on how much you linger along the way, how many detours you make into narrow lanes that seem to promise a discovery.

So let's get started. Exit at Iriya (Hibiya Line) and find the Shitaya 2-chome intersection (下谷二丁目交差点). Just before the crossing you will see a shop that specializes in twine, all kinds, shapes, and colors. If that is on your shopping list, save it for this trip.

Turn to the left. Across the street you will see the salesroom/workshop of Tadashi Kimura,[1] a carpenter-furniture maker who can perform the most delicate unions in the art of Japanese joinery. No nails are required. It is the perfect fit of interlocking pieces that distinguishes this craft, one that demonstrates its perfection in Shinto shrine architecture. Kimura-san will copy an old tansu or design a modern chest of drawers with the same dedication to detail. He will also repair your problem furniture, whether it concerns a drawer in a tiny writing box or a hibachi that requires restoring. Such shops still exist in Shitamachi regardless of the frequently heard complaint that you can't get anything fixed anymore.

Samisen players know Kimura-san. They come here to buy tiny

1. Tadashi Kimura, 3-1-1 Shitaya, Taito-ku; tel. 874–7926
   木村 正　台東区下谷 3-1-1

foldup "seats," so compact they fit in a handbag. At Kabuki performances, musicians must remain in the Japanese kneel-sit position for long periods of time, and even professionals can find it uncomfortable after a while. These tiny stands are used to take the weight of the body instead of having the burden placed on the legs alone. Unfortunately, since they are only raised a few inches from the floor, they cannot be used as auxiliary seats on commuter trains, but if you spend much time in the traditional *o-suwari* position, an *aibiki* might be useful. They are so perfect in design, so compact, so fitted for what they are supposed to do, that you may be tempted to purchase one as an outstanding example of Japanese craftsmanship and design, but be prepared for the fact that price is based on quality, not size. The wood is mulberry. In earlier days, when silk was a major Japanese product, there were many mulberry "orchards" because the leaves of the trees comprised the basic diet of the voracious silkworms. Now Japan imports most of its silk, and mulberry wood is increasing in value.

Next you will pass a doll shop, Yokoyama Ningyo-ten (横山人形店). Stop in and be greeted by the friendly proprietor. Like many Shitamachi stores, his traces its history back over several generations. Many of the dolls are made on the premises. Others are purchased from well-known *sensei,* or teachers. Each has a wooden plaque with the name of the maker.

If you want a quick and inexpensive lunch, stop at Maruka (マルカ), a new soba/tempura house with a long history. The natural wood is beautifully finished, the kind that will age well, so that years from now people will marvel at the craftsmanship of today's woodworkers.

Just beyond is a tiny shrine called Bake Jizo (化地蔵) filled with offerings: streamers of folded paper cranes, flowers in vases and Coke bottles, food, even a bright embroidered butterfly. The stone Jizo figure enshrined there commemorates a sad story.

Years ago, a certain samurai assigned directly to the shogun had a sickly wife who was always taking to her bed with one ailment or another. After a while, he was attracted to Kogiku, a young serving girl who worked in the house. The wife, jealous of the girl and angry because her husband no longer visited her to sympathize with her frail condition, lured Kogiku outside and killed her, making it appear that she had hung herself. The wife was sure she would get away with her crime because people would think the girl killed herself in remorse for her wicked behavior in seducing the husband of a sickly wife, for such, it is written, was the custom in those long-ago days.

Our scene shifts to a teacher of martial arts, so famous he had more than three thousand *deshi,* or students. He saw the girl, sitting on a stone and crying as he was returning home. He asked her why she was there, and she explained what had happened. What he was seeing was only a ghost, she said. Her body was even then dangling from a pine tree beside the road, for she had been cruelly murdered by a jealous wife.

The master hurried to the spot, but it was not the girl who was hanging there. Instead, it was the Jizo statue you see within this small shrine.

Did the god come to ease her death? Did the husband arrive in time to save his beloved and substitute the statue? Or did the girl somehow survive and devise her own revenge by telling the teacher of the "murder"? No one knows, but many come to make offerings. We can only surmise what petitions they bring. Do they ask for good health, or protection from jealous wives? This Jizo is said to be especially helpful to those who are near death, making them healthy again, which might be evidence that Kogiku survived.

There is a spectacular bathhouse on your route, Anraku-yu,[2] just past the signal light that marks a pedestrian crossing. Look up at the roof, where the steep-sloping sides are joined at a large, decorative center tile. There is the name written in kanji, and be-

2. Anraku-yu, 4–1–2 Negishi, Taito-ku; tel. 872–2662
   安楽湯　台東区根岸 4-1-2

low, at the next level, the family crest. At the corners, the two gods of happiness and prosperity, Ebisu and Daikoku, smile down at the people passing by. Inside, the high ceilings are paneled with two of Japan's most treasured woods—*hinoki,* a kind of cedar, and *keyaki,* a darker, close-grained wood that the dictionary defines as zelkova elm. This is one of only a few old-style bathhouses left in Tokyo. You will find another in Asakusa.

The building is so grandiose that you might expect it to be some lord's mansion left over from a movie set for a samurai drama rather than a *sento,* or public bath. Yet such baths have long been the gathering places for Shitamachi people. You will be welcome if you would like to have the bath experience. Expect a few curious stares at first, but the people who live in shitamachi are basically friendly, and there is no more a common denominator than nakedness, so soon you will be exchanging pleasantries. The level of involvement will depend on your language ability, but even a novice not much past *komban wa* will be able to make do with gestures and smiles.

It is rather sad to say, however, that there may not be many to share the bath with you. "People don't come any more," Ishikawa-san, the proprietor, says. "Even the smallest apartments have their own baths these days. People still like the sento, but it's more convenient to bathe at home. Times are changing."

One category of guests is increasing, he reports. TV crews, newspaper reporters, and magazine writers come in ever greater numbers to record in word and picture a fast-passing tradition.

Ishikawa-san is concerned about the future. He would like to have the fine old building preserved, but it isn't a profitable business anymore ... and he has to think of his family. He wonders if his son will want to continue the business.

The bathhouse owner lives alongside the narrow pathway that leads to the temple next door for which the bathhouse was named—Anraku-ji (安楽寺). The buildings are new but the temple's history reaches back eight hundred years. The stone marker by the door was put up by devout priests who lived there some two hundred years ago. They followed faithfully the proscriptions of Buddha against taking the life of any living creature and against carnal lust, and they wanted those who visited the temple to do the same. So please, the marker says, don't come inside if you have recently eaten fish or womanized. (No mention was made of meat because in those days hardly anyone ate it anyway.) Those admonitions are forgotten now and people come here to pray for the health and well-being of their children, with no regard for diet or leisure-time activities.

Takase[3] is the showplace of the neighborhood. Often small shops and restaurants opened their doors first in Shitamachi and, when they became successful, moved on to Ginza or other prestigious locations.

Takase just stayed, and now the Ginza trade comes to Shitamachi, for this is one of the city's finest sushi shops. You will recognize that as soon as you slide open the door. There are special straw-matted rooms—*zashiki*—for parties, and a choice of menus (you can be certain the *sashimi* course will be outstanding). There is a counter where patrons order from the day's finest fare, attractively arranged to tempt the connoisseurs—and counter customers will be rewarded occasionally with samples of delicious house specials—a cucumber sliced razer thin, touched with miso, wrapped again in cucumber and seaweed, or a crisp radish pickle. But there are no squat tables and benches for lunch-time specials, the *teishoku,* for there are none of these specials. Top sushi houses are rarely a bargain, but they are always an experience. Everything seems perfectly designed for the time and the place—the minute gardens, the little bridge that leads you across a stream to the party rooms, even the restroom—all testify to special attention.

Notice the painting of a *kappa,* the strange creature you will

3. Takase, 4–2–15 Negishi, Taito-ku; tel. 872–0129
　　高勢　台東区根岸 4-2-15

meet later at Kappabashi. The present owner (his grandfather founded the shop) will tell you that in the old days all sushi shops displayed kappa somewhere. It was a sign of the *mizu shobai* world, the world of nighttime entertainment.

As you leave, don't miss the picturesque red lanterns near the entryway. Until recently, similar lanterns were a familiar sight in this area. They were put up by the shopkeepers to retain a look of the past. Most of them were removed in a recent street-repair project, and only these two remain. They cast a pleasant glow in the evening, alongside the willow tree.

There is another pleasant surprise in Negishi, a French restaurant, Kamiya (香味屋). If you are uncomfortable with the unposted prices at Takase, this could be your choice. This shop too is a third-generation establishment. It first opened its doors in Taisho 14, or 1925, and is one of the oldest Western restaurants in Tokyo. The name as it is read in Japanese encompasses the elements of good cooking: aroma and flavor. People come here from all over Tokyo, the owner will tell you. "However, we retain the old-time feeling," he continues. "Our guests can come in everyday dress, shoes or geta. It doesn't matter."

Watch for the tofu shop, Komatsuya (小松屋). They make their own bean curd and have some distinctive specialities. There are also a variety of fish-paste products. Prices are quite low, the foods are nutritious, and you may even find them delicious. It's a good place to experiment.

Next, another old-time shop. As you walk along watch for the double-doored entrance to Ebiya Some Kojo (海老屋染工場), a home factory that preserves an old art, the dyeing of fabrics. Women select patterns for their silk kimono. Gardeners and tradesmen come to have the symbols of their trade dyed on the blue cotton *happi* coats that most of them still wear.

Now there is a tea-cake shop to visit, a place where you will wonder how sweets can become such works of art. Okano Eisen (岡埜榮泉) too has a long history if you trace it back to its origin.

The owner earned the right to his *noren,* the short curtain that hangs over the door, from his teacher, a master maker of tea cakes. Notice the *furoshiki* that are used instead of bags for some of the gift wrappings. They are as strong as cloth, but they are paper. Also look at the wrapping paper that pictures an old temple beneath a gigantic pine, a stream gently flowing beneath its wide-spread branches. Soon you will see what's left of that scene—at Ogyo no Matsu (お行の松). Hiroshige was certainly not the first to record that corner of old Edo, but his woodblock print, the one you saw reproduced on the wrapping paper at Okano Eisen, is famous as part of his series *One Hundred Edo Views*. The pine tree stood in the garden of a small temple for more than three hundred years and was a landmark for the whole area, much as Tokyo Tower is for modern Tokyo. (There is a rumor that even Tokyo Tower will shortly make way for change in this most change-able of all cities, that with more modern means of broadcasting now available, it will be torn down so its valuable land may be put to more profitable use. *O tempora! O mores!*)

A piece of the first pine is on display beside the new one, the third, barely started, growing beside it in a corner garden. The second was planted around 1928 and soon died. Nor is the new one growing well, and there is a marker where visitors can pause and wish for a strong tree once more to shade this site. It is not likely to happen. The story is told how the stream beneath the first tree was drained, and afterward, as the people watched in sad surprise, it died "very quickly."

You will see the old pine again, in the Kappabashi chapter, at the memorial museum that commemorates the life of Ichiyo Higuchi, a woman writer of the Meiji era, who lived in the neigh-borhood and wrote romantic novels about its people.

The small temple houses a Fudo deity. The square stagelike plaform with exotic paraphernalia is used for performing *goma,* or purification, ceremonies. You will learn more about this rite in the Narita chapter.

There was no Alcoholics Anonymous in the old days. Perhaps that is why a neighborhood group got together at Enko-ji temple (円光寺), our next stop, to pray that family members and friends who overindulged in sakè would somehow be cured of their desire to drink. This group offered prayers to a god who sits on a sakè barrel, symbolically keeping it from being opened. His shrine is down a narrow pathway in front of the temple gate. You too can ask for help (for yourself, for a friend) at Enko-ji, also known as Fuji-dera because of its lavish display of wisteria (*fuji*) blossoms in the spring. One huge vine is known to be more than two hundred years old.

We don't know if anyone was cured by their prayers, but their offerings helped continue the drinking habits of the *furosha,* vagrants, who made their homes in doorways and station passages in the Ueno-Asakusa area. Perhaps because of the temple's close association with alcohol, many people included sakè along with the flowers they brought as offerings to the deceased in the adjacent cemetery. And at night the furosha would come and drink whatever they could find. Now there is a sign asking people not to leave liquor offerings.

There is a small shrine to the right that once housed six small Jizo figures, but they have been taken inside for safer keeping. "This was once a poor neighborhood," the priest explains. "Gardeners and carpenters lived here, and many of their children died when they were babies. Also, Yoshiwara, the old pleasure quarter, was nearby, and few of the babies of the girls who worked there survived. These poor infants were all alone, there was no one to help them get across the river that separates this world from the other, so these Jizo statues were given the responsibility. The poor people would pray that the six Jizo would help their babies find their way to paradise." (Jizo, a Buddhist deity, is popularly regarded as the guardian of children and pregnant women.)

Enko-ji is a little out of the way, hidden among the back streets, but it is well worth the effort of seeking it out. You will feel that you have escaped from Tokyo and found an almost-forgotten refuge in some far away place. It is surrounded, almost overwhelmed, by flowers and greenery depending on the season, and it is quite apparent that no gardener has coaxed each branch into its proper place. Many Japanese gardens have a contrived "naturalness" that is achieved only with tremendous effort. Here, the garden just is.

You might pass by Saizo-in (西蔵院), it looks so new, so modern, but it has a history of more than four hundred years. If you walk behind the temple building, you will discover a beautiful Japanese-style garden. This is the temple that looks after the new Ogyo no Matsu, the pine tree that would seem to need all the help it can get.

As you leave, walk through the memorial ground to the left. You will see a mound of stone carvings. Many people are buried here, vagrants, the homeless, those whom no one claimed. People leave offerings, and ceremonies are held for them, asking that their spirits may find peace. Behind the mound is a memorial to a famous craftsman, Murata, maker of *kiseru,* the old-style Japanese pipe which held only a pinch of tobacco.

By now it is apparent that there are many temples in this area. You have probably paused now and then to admire a roof's gentle curve or a garden's striking arrangement of rocks and pines. Sometimes you may have peered inside for a glimpse of the deity enshrined within, but rarely will you know of the treasures that a temple may hold. Here is just one example.

Eisho-ji (永稱寺). Yes, here you would pause to admire the sweeping roof, the trees and rocks. You could try to see within the temple, but the view would be dim and unrewarding. How could you know that there is a marvelous screen of a tiger peering through the bamboo, a sly smile on his face as if he feels that he really can hide behind those slender stalks. The artist, whom the temple brochure identifies as Kano Sukoku, created a playful-looking tiger, and wherever you stand, the animal seems to be looking directly at you. The temple also has a famous kakemono, a hanging scroll, showing a phoenix on a golden background, attributed to Kano Yusen. The phoenix is the legendary bird that could rise from the fires that engulfed it. This scroll missed such a fiery death in World War II, when it was hidden away before the bombs fell. Unfortunately, these masterpieces are not on public view, but at least you know they are there. I asked the caretaker about these treasures. He shrugged slightly. "The whole temple is a treasure," he said. So don't regret that you can't see the screen and the scroll and look at the treasure that surrounds you.

The temple is sometimes called Hato-dera (pigeon temple) because of the flocks of these birds that inhabit the grounds. It is also known for scissors and you will see a stone monument with a carving of a pair of scissors. It memorializes one Yakichi, a maker of scissors, a trade that his family continues today. Each spring, there is a scissors fair along the walk that leads to the temple. Most are still made by hand.

Our last temple on this block is Senju-in (千手院), where you can slide open a tiny window in the door in front of the worship hall and see the Buddha with a thousand arms that is enshrined within. It is obvious that the statue does not have that many arms, but the number is only symbolic.

A well-known tea-ceremony teacher gives lessons at the temple, and occasionally there is a special ceremony for worn-out *chasen* —tea whisks made of split bamboo—in the garden behind the main building. You will see a stone marker just beyond the bamboo fence that marks the place where they are solemnly burned.

You have reached an intersection. If you would like another small diversion, cross at the signal light and take the narrow street beyond the *sembei* shop that goes back toward the site of Hiroshige's pine. There are small shops, more temples, and the opportunity to speculate on just what home industry is being performed in the workshops you can see inside some of the buildings.

Or you can continue along the same street. You will be passing little shops, many of which have been modernized. There is one selling tortoise-shell ornaments including tiny butterfly pins at small prices, and, not surprisingly, a sushi shop. (There is always a sushi shop.) But back away and look at the upper story. It appears to be much older than the shops that line the street. The building is said to be Tokyo's second "modern" apartment building, built shortly after the 1923 earthquake. The first apartment development is on Omotesando, near Harajuku Station. Those buildings have weathered better. But then, they were far more luxurious. The Shitamachi apartments provide space for a small shop, a multi-purpose room behind, and a tiny kitchen. Toilet facilities are communal, and the bath is not down the hall; it is down the street at one of the neighborhood bathhouses. A novelist once chose this building as the setting for his story about Shitamachi.

But perhaps there will be some new *apato* (apartment building) there when you make your visit. The ninety-year-old owner died recently. If the usual pattern is followed, the property will be sold and a new building constructed. But there will be similar buildings. Look across almost any street for a better view of the first-floor shops and the second-floor or in-the-back residences. This once-common living arrangement for shop owners has hung on a little longer in Shitamachi. Some of the buildings seem so tired and worn that you wonder, should the wind blow a little harder, if they might not collapse and bring down this small remaining picturesque view of yesterday. It probably isn't necessary to add that while the new apartments are certainly not as "picturesque," they are far more comfortable for those who live in them.

Across the street are two sembei stores. The rice crackers are made on the premises, and you will discover some new varieties. One may surprise you because of its deep, black color. Don't be misled. It is neither chocolate nor seaweed. It is a coating made from black sugar, the old-style unrefined variety. At Azumaya (あづまや), the proprietor will tell you of the history of the shop now more than a hundred years old. The original building survived the Great Kanto Earthquake in 1923 and the bombing of World War II that leveled much of the city around it, but it could not withstand modernization and was a victim of a recent street-widening program.

And finally, one more temple, this one Yoden-ji. Or Hoju-zan. It has two names. (要伝寺，法住山) As the priest's wife explained, all temples should be built on mountains. If there is no mountain to build it on, then it is given a mountain name. The second name includes the character for "mountain" (it is read *zan*) and it serves as a substitute for the real thing.

Hoyu-zan makes the most of what space it has. "Gradually it has become smaller," she says, explaining that with every street-widening project the temple loses a bit more of its land. Today the temple compound is only half its former size.

Now you have completed your stroll through Negishi. If you turn left, a few minutes' walk will bring you once again to Iriya subway station. Watch for it on the left. Slightly before, across the street, you will see the steeply slanting roof of Kishibojin (鬼子母神), the temple where the famous morning-glory festival is held in early July. (See Uguisudani chapter, *Foot-loose in Tokyo*.) Or take the Yamanote Line from Uguisudani Station only a short walk away.

"Negishi? There is nothing there," people might tell you, and in a way it is true. A sushi shop, a French restaurant, a doll maker, a temple. . . . You will find them anywhere. And yet there is a difference for those who like to recapture at least a small touch of the past.

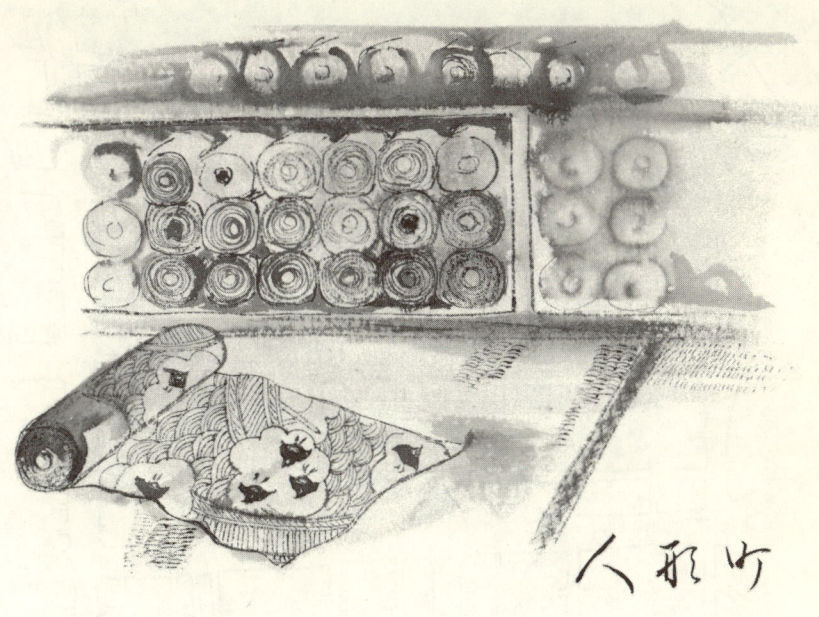

人形町

Ningyo-cho: Doll Town

THE NEXT SURFACING from the subway could be Ningyo-cho. We orient from the Hibiya Line, but you could also take the Toei Asakusa Line. The word *ningyo* means "doll," so you might expect to find doll makers clustered in this area. There are none now, but some 350 years ago there were several Bunraku theaters here, and the dolls that were manipulated on stage by black-shrouded handlers were made nearby. Children's dolls were another product, and special doll markets were held several times a year.

None of this remains, but there is a famous theater in Ningyo-cho, the Meiji-za, founded in 1893, in the Meiji era. It is remark-

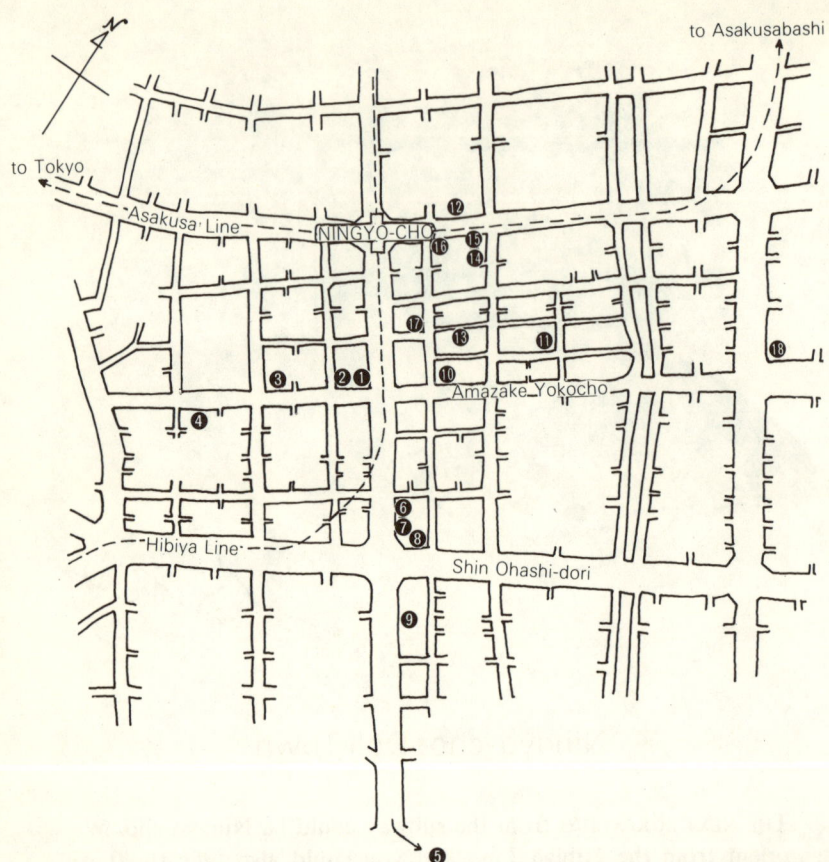

1. Kaisei-ken
2. Tamahide
3. Uokyu
4. Tokyo Grain Exchange
5. TCAT
6. Kotobuki-do
7. Kofujiya
8. Shigemori
9. Suitengu
10. Iwai Shoten
11. Geigiya Kumiai
12. Hamadaya
13. Homi-tei
14. Yoneyama
15. Obase Orimono
16. Kyotaru
17. Hiyama
18. Meiji-za

able for its perseverence. Copying the legendary *ho-o* bird, the phoenix, it continues to rise from its ashes. Like most of the neighborhood, the theater was leveled during World War II though it had survived, as few others had, the massive 1923 earthquake. But the postwar building burned too and was once more rebuilt in 1958. Today's building looks solid enough to last. The park in front extends to the Sumida River, where you can watch the barges and water taxis go by; or you can walk along the cement river embankment with a complex network of overhead highways shading you from the sun. How different from the days when lanterns lit the paths along the river and sounds of the samisen could be heard from the teahouses where people stopped for refreshments.

You will find a more modern teahouse near the subway exit though it now specializes in coffee. Kaisei-ken[1] is identified by a figure of a cow above the door. The reason: the owner was born in the zodiac year of the ox. However, you are more likely to notice the bean-shaped *mokugyo,* a hollow, wooden, clapperless "bell." Buddhist priests strike these objects with a mallet as they recite sutras. You will see them often in temples.

This was one of Tokyo's first Western teahouses, one that featured "British" tea. It was quite in contrast to the Japanese teahouse image of a place where people ate and drank and perhaps made arrangements for the evening's entertainment. Kaisei-ken first opened its doors in 1919. Then the hot summer air was stirred by a new innovation, a ceiling fan. It is still there, though more modern methods are now used for heating and cooling. A few of the family treasures are on display, one a lance from old samurai days which suggests a cross in the design. Christianity was supported in the Sendai area, the ancestral home of the owners. If you wonder what their ancestor looked like, check the mask on the

---

1. Kaisei-ken, 1–17–19, Ningyo-cho, Chuo-ku; tel. 669–0880
   快生軒　中央区人形町 1-17-19

wall. It was made from a part of the great center-post that supported the roof beam of the family homestead back in Sendai. It is said to be carved in the likeness of the family founder.

Should you stop here for morning coffee, you will see many of the local residents who drop in to read the newspapers provided for them. For a few moments, as you drink your coffee, you can feel that you are a part of the Shitamachi community.

Note Tamahide,[2] the restaurant on the next corner, where you may want to have lunch. The sign in front tells you how the original owner, seven generations ago, was in service to the shogun. It was he who was called to prepare the cranes for the ruler's crane stew, a favorite dish at the shogun's palace in those days. It is said that he was so deft with his knives that he could perform his art without touching the birds with his hands, and without any visible sign of blood.

The restaurant also claims to have devised the first serving of a lunch-time favorite, *oyako domburi* (rice topped with a chicken-and-egg mixture simmered in a tasty sauce). The name means "parent" (the chicken) and "child" (the egg). While many of you may have tried oyako domburi before, the traditional version served here in red-lacquer bowls will be a pleasant surprise. The special *teishoku* (fixed-menu meal) is served only from 11:30 A.M. to 1 P.M., and is reasonably priced for such generous servings. At many restaurants it is hard to find the "parent" in the oyako domburi. At night, the menu lists various special courses, most featuring chicken. Reservations are recommended. It is a nice place to take friends to demonstrate your knowledge of old Tokyo.

On down the street, on the second floor of an old and attractive Japanese-style building, is Uokyu,[3] a restaurant with a different specialty: fish. Ningyo-cho has been known for many years for its

2. Tamahide, 1–17–10 Ningyo-cho, Chuo-ku; tel. 668–7651
   玉ひで　中央区人形町 1-17-10
3. Uokyu, 1–1–20 Ningyo-cho, Chuo-ku; tel. 666–2869
   魚久　中央区人形町 1-1-20

way with fish both cooked and raw. Here the claim is well demonstrated. On the corner, and a part of the same enterprise, is a sushi restaurant where each portion served is a miniature work of art. Ask for the house specialty, *gindara*, fish flavored in sakè mash for several days before cooking, a different and delicious taste experience that is distinctly Japanese.

Across the street you will see an imposing structure, its gray pillars contrasting with the familiar buildings of old and new Japan that surround it. The nameplate tells us it is the Tokyo Grain Exchange (東京穀物取引所) and indeed it was, in earlier days, but today its mission is beans. Here, under the domed ceiling in the central exchange hall, transactions in soy beans and other imported beans that make up a large part of the nation's diet are carried out.

It is likely that the style of the building is no accident. Rome's stock exchange is housed in an ancient temple. Early architects must have felt that the design was appropriate, and throughout the world, exchanges of many kinds are marked by columned fronts. Unlike many of the world's great cities, Tokyo can claim little that is truly old. Even its ancient shrines are periodically rebuilt, the "ancient" denoting only the style, which is re-created in minute detail. This building, however, is old in the Japanese sense; it has stood here for half a century. But its Western style ends on the roof. There you can see a miniature Shinto shrine.

Returning to the main street and crossing the intersection, you will see a network of overhead highways a few blocks to the right. They mark the entrance of TCAT (Tokyo City Air Terminal), the bus center for Narita airport passengers at Hakozaki. But that is not included on today's tour. Head in that direction, however. Along the way, you will notice two shops featuring attractive maternity clothes; you will know why a few paragraphs later.

If you don't watch for it, you might miss Kotobukido,[4] a tiny,

4. Kotobukido, 2–1–4 Ningyo-cho, Chuo-ku; tel. 666–4804
   寿堂　中央区人形町 2-1-4

time-faded shop, but you will probably notice the crowd of customers, mostly women, waiting in line to buy sweet bean-cakes, the almost-too-pretty-to-eat variety served with Japanese tea. Some, like the perfect replica of a fish on a bed of salt displayed in the window, must be ordered in advance. Note the old clock on the wall, its face in the style of early time-telling in Japan.

A few doors beyond is Kofujiya,[5] a shop specializing in sembei rice crackers. There are samples for tasting, and you will probably discover several new favorites, available at bargain prices.

On the corner is Shigemori,[6] a good place to sample *ningyo-yaki*. These bean-paste-filled confections are a traditional product of the area. You can look behind the curtains into the back room where people are busily filling small waffle-iron-like molds with batter and beans.

Continue along the street for the explanation of why Ningyo-cho features maternity clothes. Notice first that the street lamps resemble little lanterns, designed to make the night scene more festive for the famous shrine they mark. The shop at the entrance-way would be a child's delight, all kinds of handmade candies with patterns of faces and flowers. They are purchased as appropriate gifts, for Suitengu (水天宮) is the shrine where people come to ask the gods to watch over a mother-to-be and her baby.

It is not necessary for the pregnant woman to come herself, though usually you will see a few young couples ringing one of the bells in front of the shrine. It is quite all right for parents or grandparents to make the request. (In fact, today this is often the way; modern girls are not as likely to seek out traditional safeguards, being more inclined to rely on national health insurance.) And quite often they will take home a gift—a long cotton obi that in the old days was wound around the abdomen for added protection

5. Kofujiya, 2–1–3 Ningyo-cho, Chuo-ku; tel. 669–7733
   小藤屋　中央区人形町 2-1-3
6. Shigemori, 2–1–1 Ningyo-cho, Chuo-ku; tel. 666–5885
   重盛　中央区人形町 2-1-1

from the fifth month of pregnancy. This was best done on the zodiac day of the dog, for dogs have easy deliveries. Few girls wear these *hara-obi* now; they require kimono, not Western dress. Still, many people will buy them because they are traditional; in such matters as babies, it is best to take no chances.

Notice, too, the bells hanging in front of the shrine. Five are provided, an indication of the number of people who visit here. Usually a bell is shaken vigorously to call the attention of the gods to the petition. Here a sign instructs visitors to pull straight down on the rope, for this is the best pathway for a safe and easy delivery.

Anchors are worked into the designs of the lanterns that stand in front of the shrine and others are displayed nearby. The sea once reached near this spot, and the shrine had the additional mission of protecting any who had involvements with water. Of course this was mainly intended for fishermen, but it was far broader in its interpretation. It was said that a *mamori* (an amulet) purchased at the shrine office offered protection from such minor tragedies as having one's clothing splashed with muddy water from a speeding rickshaw.

Look along the walls for old photos that show some of the early shrine festivals. Today's crowds seem almost sparse in comparison. And look behind the shrine for another example of how things change. Certainly there is money still to be made from selling hara-obi, and people still toss coins in the money box in front of the shrine, but the fees paid by those who park their cars in the garage over which the present shrine is built provide a steady income. Even old shrines with traditional missions must find ways to cope with today's economic challenges.

Now, back to the main intersection. This time turn right, passing in front of a shop selling tea. Even if you don't see it, you will be aware of the slightly acrid, pleasant aroma. Next a shop displaying tofu, many varieties, and usually a line of housewives waiting to make their selections. On the corner, a weaver, this one of bamboo.

Iwai-san[7] weaves thin strips of bamboo into covered baskets that are then lacquered. The Japanese have used these *kori* for hundreds of years. They fit easily into Japanese closets, where things are folded, not hung. Storing clothing in kori tends to prevent mildew, a constant problem in humid Japan. Order one with your family crest in a choice of colors—black or Chinese red.

Pass a samisen maker, a shop featuring boxed lunches, and turn to find the headquarters of the local geisha organization, Yoshi-cho Geigiya Kumiai.[8] There are still geisha houses in Ningyo-cho. One, Hamadaya,[9] would rival the finest in more fashionable areas. Walk by and look at the exquisite entrance garden, but don't stop in for dinner unless you are prepared to pay more than twenty thousand yen per person for your enjoyment of *kaiseki ryori,* or formal banquet-type food served in the traditional manner. This means that what is presented may be more appealing to the eye than to the palate, at least from the Western point of view.

There are not so many geisha in Ningyo-cho today, and of the twenty or so who are left, each will have counted at least fifty years. Now they have a union, and regular days off. The headquarters building is used for neighborhood entertainments. If you are there on a Saturday, you may hear laughter from an upstairs room. There are occasional performances of *rakugo,* comic story tellers, and other old-time artists such as *kamikiriya,* who cut amusing figures from paper as they tell stories designed to entertain.

By now you will have noted that Ningyo-cho's streets are lined with traditional eating places. You are not far from one of the most interesting—look for a faded sign with "Restaurant" written in English. That is the only indication that this eating-house, too, is

7. Iwai Shoten, 2–10–1 Ningyo-cho, Chuo-ku; tel. 668–6058
   岩井商店　中央区人形町 2-10-1
8. Yoshi-cho Geigiya Kumiai, 2–22–9 Ningyo-cho, Chuo-ku; tel. 666–5966
   芳町芸妓屋組合　中央区人形町 2-22-9
9. Hamadaya, 3–13 Ningyo-cho, Chuo-ku; tel. 661–5435
   浜田屋　中央区人形町 3-13

not specializing in some Japanese delicacy. For this is Homi-tei,[10] one of Tokyo's early Western-style restaurants. It still follows the original style: though the menu is Western, the service is very Japanese. Most guests choose to sit at low tables on the tatami floor, eating their beef stew or steaks or sole meunière with their choice of chopsticks or knife and fork. You will see many families "eating out" at Homi-tei, perhaps experiencing the feeling of something foreign even though it is just around the corner from home.

The first chefs contributed their own international expertise— they had all worked on NYK Line ships. (The restaurant has always been favored by men of the sea.) Today's chef received his international experience from a different source—the Foreign Correspondents' Club of Japan.

Two short blocks away and you will step back into the past at Yoneyama,[11] a rice dealer whose house and shop claim almost a century of history. Even today, an old rice-polishing machine is at work at the back of the storehouse. The owner recalls World War II when this area was burned—to his street. "Thanks to the wide street and the Sumida River, we were saved," he recalls. The fire burned almost everything up to his shop, but he was protected from the flames. The old building next door also survived. Then it was a geisha house. Now it belongs to a dentist.

Other shops survived the bombings, among them Obase Orimono a kimono dealer. The shop is the same, a tatami-covered raised platform for showing the rolls of silk fabric, while the customer sat alongside selecting favorites. Only today, if it is evening, the family car will be parked where the customers once sat admiring the fabrics. Overnight street parking is illegal in Japan. In fact, when buying a car, one must have a document signed by the local police

10. Homi-tei, 2–9–4 Ningyo-cho, Chuo-ku; tel. 666–5687
    芳味亭　中央区人形町 2-9-4
11. Yoneyama, 2–7–12 Ningyo-cho, Chuo-ku; tel. 666–5850
    米山　中央区人形町 2-7-12

office stating that an off-street parking space is available. Thus many shops also double as garages.

"Come in July," the proprietor says. "Then we have *Bon odori* (folk dancing) in the park. And in August, on the fifth and sixth, we have a chinaware fair. In the old days, there were many china manufacturers here." Some of them made ceramic figures that were sold at the early doll markets. They can still be found occasionally at antique stores and flea markets.

Turn the corner for an old-style sushi shop, Kyotaru,[12] specializing in the "wrapped" kind, neat little bundles filled with rice and seasonal delicacies. At the back, under the same roof, is an elegant restaurant featuring kaiseki foods.

Turning again, and back on the main street, you will see Hiyama, (日山) a sukiyaki restaurant priding itself on serving the tenderest beef and the freshest vegetables.

If you cross the street—look for the arch and a huge lantern that mark the entrance to a Kannon temple—you will find even more restaurants, a narrow lane lined with appealing shops. Slide open a doorway and try to guess what's being served.

Or—should your choice be to explore the old streets of Ningyo-cho, look to the right for what was once Yoshiwara, the "gay quarters" of early Edo. Later this center for prostitution was moved to an area near Asakusa, where it flourished as the floating world of pleasure depicted in woodblock prints. Today little in the area of warehouses and wholesale showrooms, and an occasional house in what appears to be Meiji style, holds even a reminder of those days. You will learn more of this "transient world" in the Yoshiwara chapter.

Or you could walk past the sukiyaki restaurant along the main street, noticing the variety of merchandise for sale—zori, handbags, T-shirts, neckties, umbrellas, children's clothes, fabrics—until

12. Kyotaru, 2–7–5 Ningyo-cho, Chou-ku; tel. 668–7111
京樽　中央区人形町 2-7-5

you reach the corner where you started your exploration of Nin-gyo-cho. Turn left at this intersection if you want to visit the Meiji-za theater,[13] its many flags rippling in the breezes from the Sumida River and its gigantic pictures of Kabuki performers making it impossible to miss.

If you are sturdy and the weather is fine, you could stroll along the river to our next stop, Asakusabashi, but should you choose this path, your view will be mostly concrete embankments. Your imagination must supply the lantern-lined path and the cherry blossoms of olden days.

Edo residents traveled this way: on foot. They had no choice. You, however, can also go by subway or walk along the main street. You will pass many shops that will catch your interest, for this is the great Tokyo wholesale area. Almost everything that you have ever wanted will be on sale somewhere along the busy streets of Shitamachi.

But you may choose to stay a little longer in Ningyo-cho, where history lingers on. Listen, and you may hear a haunting melody being played on a samisen or a *shakuhachi,* a bamboo flute. Look-ing down a narrow street, you may see an old, especially attractive house, a dainty name-sign by the door, a miniature garden at the entrance. Perhaps some geisha has chosen this old part of Tokyo for her home. That old warehouse—was it someone's residence in Meiji days? Did children play daimyo and court lady behind those dormer windows?

Today, we can only guess, but speculation is also a part of the pleasure of traveling back in time to the streets of Edo.

13. Meiji-za, 2–31–1 Hama-cho, Chuo-ku; tel. 667–5151
明治座　中央区浜町 2-31-1

Asakusabashi and Kuramae:
Sparse Grass Bridge and At the Storehouse

OUR PREVIOUS STOP, Ningyo-cho, was named for dolls. It seems that the name should have been given to Asakusabashi instead, for the station area abounds with doll shops. You will see the traditional type, the samurai and the lady, along with cute romping babies, dancers, and geisha waiting for their patrons. There are also Western dolls, most in what is assumed to be the finery of the old South, huge skirts with cascading ruffles, parasols, and auburn or blonde hair. All come in glass cases to keep them pretty and clean for generations, for these dolls are not to be played with, they are only for decoration. Some of the stores, like

Kyugetsu,[1] provide doll-making classes; some, like Kuramae Ningyo-sha,[2] sell the tiny accessories that are essential to the well-turned-out creation. During the summer, lanterns become a part of the doll-store trade. Most are made of *washi* (handmade paper), thin and delicate and decorated with graceful pictures of the seven fall grasses. For years such lanterns have welcomed the return of the spirits of the ancestors at the celebration of Obon.

Some of the shops have diversified even further. Shugetsu,[3] for example, features clothing and accessories made of traditional fabrics, and a Japanese teahouse-like restaurant.

The teahouse look is appropriate, for this was once an area filled with such places. It was here that many patrons waited for boats to transport them to Yoshiwara, where they would lose themselves in the "floating world of pleasure." Some never got beyond Asakusabashi's hospitality, however, for the waitresses here were also known for their charming ways. Some maintain that they were the real forerunners of today's geisha.

People no longer dally along the streets of Asakusabashi, for this is a busy wholesale district with thousands of shops and distributors trying to gain a share of the business.

However, as you walk along the canal, you will note that the boats are still there. Today they take fishermen out into Tokyo Bay, or you can make arrangements for private parties where guests will be served beer and sakè and freshly prepared tempura as the boat glides through the channel and out into the river, truly a modern "floating world of pleasure" on a summer night.

On the left you will pass a shop selling bean-paste confections. You might wonder at the number of these specialty shops. Surely they indicate that Japanese are loyal to their traditional sweets.

1. Kyugetsu, 1–20–4 Yanagibashi, Taito-ku; tel. 861–5511
   久月　台東区柳橋 1-20-4
2. Kuramae Ningyo-sha, 4–14–4 Kuramae, Taito-ku; tel. 861–5458
   蔵前人形社　台東区蔵前 4-14-4
3. Shugetsu, 1–20–3 Yanagibashi, Taito-ku; tel. 861–8801
   秀月　台東区柳橋 1-20-3

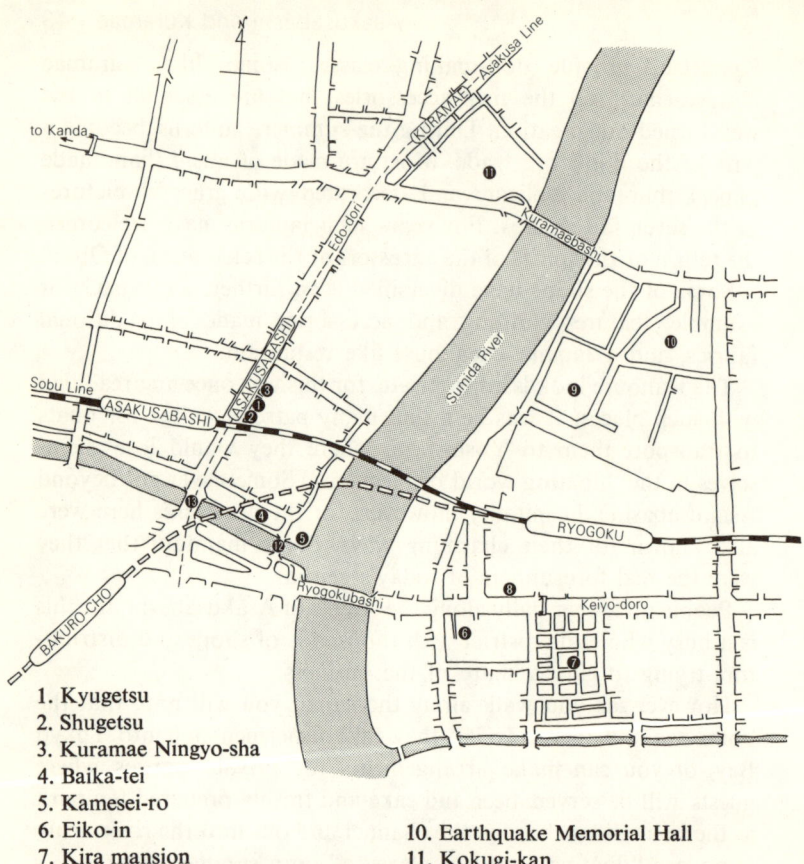

1. Kyugetsu
2. Shugetsu
3. Kuramae Ningyo-sha
4. Baika-tei
5. Kamesei-ro
6. Eiko-in
7. Kira mansion
8. Tomoegata
9. Yasuda Teien Park
10. Earthquake Memorial Hall
11. Kokugi-kan
12. Yanagibashi
13. Asakusabashi

This is a branch store of one of the most famous, Baika-tei (梅花亭), located on the other side of the river, which counts back fifteen generations to its founding. You can look into the back room and see the cookie-like shells being filled with the sweet bean-paste. You might even meet the eighty-three-year-old proprietor. If you understand Japanese, he may tell you stories of the past when, as we continuously say, things were very different from today.

At the end of the street in a modern brick building, an old tradition is continued. It is here, at Kamesei-ro,[4] where sumo officials gather when major decisions, such as naming a new grand champion, are being considered. The building looks Western, but the room they meet in is Japanese traditional, with a view of the river below. Once the meetings were held in a rambling, geisha-style restaurant on this same site. Seven generations of proprietors have made arrangements for these gatherings. If you want to know what it looked like before, see the reproduction of an old woodblock print in the restaurant's brochure. Surely some monumental decision affecting sumo is being made as guests feast on what must have been the freshest of sashimi.

You too can eat there, and your choices are pictured in the brochure. Most famous is the Yanagibashi *obento,* a boxed lunch (the box a lovely, compartmented lacquer container), with the specialties of which the house is justifiably proud.

The obento is named for Yanagibashi (Willow Bridge) which spans the Kanda River and shares the corner with the restaurant. Cross it and turn right to Ryogoku Bridge (両国橋). The name in Japanese, meaning "two countries," clearly defines its role in earlier days: it linked the two provinces known as Musashi and Shimofusa. These days few people analyze the meaning of the word.

But in ancient times there was no bridge. People who needed to cross the river waited for a boatman to ferry them across—and on one tragic day in 1657 there were not enough boats to meet the demand. That was the day of horror when flames devastated the city of Edo and 108,000 people died. Thousands perished on the riverbank, trying to flee from the flames. The first bridge was built

4. Kamesei-ro, 1–1–3 Yanagibashi, Taito-ku; tel. 851–3101
　　亀清楼　台東区柳橋 1-1-3

two years after that tragic Great Furisode Fire. (See Sugamo chapter in *Foot-loose in Tokyo*.)

In July, the bridge is a popular place for viewing a magnificent fireworks display. Since Edo days, people have enjoyed watching *hanabi* ("fire flowers") as their boats floated down the Sumida River, or from a vantage point on the shore. The first festival was held in 1733 to bring peace to the spirits of all who had been lost at sea and to petition the gods to end an epidemic that was spreading throughout the city. The double-header seemed to have pleased the gods, for the epidemic abated and one assumes that the god of the sea, to whom the petition was addressed, brought peace to those he had claimed. The fireworks festival has been repeated almost every year except for a few years during Japan's rapid-growth period. Then the streets were too crowded, it was said. It was too dangerous. Now streets have been widened and new high-rise buildings have replaced small home-industry shacks, and the fireworks displays are once again an eagerly awaited summer extravaganza. We should add that thousands await them. The streets are as jammed, and the skies as alight with fire as they must have been on that dreadful night in 1657 when Edo was destroyed in the Great Furisode Fire.

A temple, Eko-in （回向院）, on the other side of the bridge, its entrance marked by a row of distinctive "daimyo" bamboo, is dedicated to those who lost their lives in that fire, and in other tragedies. The temple itself was destroyed twice—in the 1923 earthquake and in World War II. Reading the memorial markers is to share the sorrows of the past. "People who died at sea." "To aborted infants." "Ninety unclaimed citizens from the 1923 earthquake." "Those who died in prison." One, from 1895, notes that "fifty yen has been provided for eternal maintenance."

Behind the small wooden altar building is a memorial to the Japanese Robin Hood, Nezumi Kozo Jirokichi. Today you can follow his adventures on television. The two small monuments bear cuts from many knives: gamblers slip into the grounds and chip away at the stones, for it is believed that even a tiny fragment will assure good luck in their profession.

To the left of the entrance is another type of memorial. Here are stored the ashes of beloved pets, mainly dogs, cats, and birds. Go inside the building to see the stacked lockers, each decorated with a bouquet of dusty plastic flowers and often a photograph. The altar is covered with appropriate gifts: cat food, rubber bones, dog biscuits, and plastic balls. The *sotoba* (nameboards) in front indicate the variety of pet names. Here they are, remembering Charming, Poppy, Poochie, Mellon, Mimi, Rocky, Devil, Oscar. One bears no names, only the fact that it commemorates the animals that have "given" their lives in hospital experiments.

The large round building next door, which looks at first glance as if it were only recently completed, is scheduled for destruction. Now it is used by Nihon University when a huge hall is required, say at graduation time. In the past, it was the old Kokugikan, or sumo stadium. It was sold to the university when the new one was built near Kuramae. Now that one too will soon be demolished. Tokyo has little sentiment for its historic buildings.

But it is sentimental about its past. Use the side exit from the temple and go almost to the end of the street. You will see an old stone wall on the left, built to commemorate the site of the Kira mansion (吉良屋敷), where the forty-seven *ronin* finally claimed vengeance for the death of their master, Lord Asano. (See Shinagawa chapter in *Foot-loose in Tokyo*.)

Lord Kira lived in style. His house counted eight hundred *tsubo* (approximately 2,640 square meters) and the land space was 2,500 tsubo (8,250 square meters). The old well where the loyal retainers washed the severed head of their enemy is still there. There is also a small memorial shrine to the twenty men who were killed in their unsuccessful defense of Lord Kira. In area it must be one of Tokyo's smallest parks, but the story it commemorates is probably known to every Japanese. And if the walking tour is beginning to tire you a bit, remember that the samurai carried Lord Kira's head all the way to their master's grave at Sengaku-ji, near Shina-gawa Station. As has been pointed out before, in those days, people walked; long distances were accepted as normal. There was no choice. News also traveled slowly. Edo, fast asleep behind closed *amado* (sliding wooden shutters) would not know of the vendetta's conclusion until long after the dawn of the next day.

Turn left at the corner and go along to the main street. You will pass an old concrete building. It was the warehouse of the first wholesale dealer in photographic material, a business that still continues today, some one hundred years later.

Now, walking away from the temple, look down a side street for a sign in hiragana that says *chanko*. We never want you to be hungry on these excursions, and here you can try food that the giant sumo wrestlers eat, though it is doubtful that you could handle the quantity they consume. Tomoegata[5] was established by a retired sumo great. Now it is run by his son. It can accommodate large groups if you want to give a party, or you can stop in alone for lunch or dinner. There is a picture menu so you can point to order. *Chanko-nabe* is a stew. There is no recipe to restrict what to put in; just about anything goes.

Next is Ryogoku Station (両国駅), now almost deserted. Once it was the terminal for the Sobu Line. Now the tracks continue on to Tokyo Station, and the huge complex of echoing buildings seems haunted by the past, like a run-down deserted house in the middle of Tokyo's modern business district. But perhaps that is not what you will see. Perhaps you will see the splendid new sumo stadium that will one day be located here. Then the crowds will once again come to Ryogoku, and there will be no ghosts lingering in the empty rooms waiting for trains that no longer arrive.

Many sumo stables are located in this area, and if you walk the back streets behind the station, you may see young sumo-san in

5. Tomoegata, 2–17 Ryogoku, Sumida-ku; tel. 632–5600
   巴潟　墨田区両国 2-17

yukata, their hair drawn up in the prescribed knot, out for a stroll, or if you are lucky, one of today's greats. Most stables have arranged the windows of their practice halls so that the curious can look inside. Watching even a few minutes of the training will impress you with the tremendous strength and resistance that must be developed by these giant wrestlers.

Next, Yasuda Teien Park (安田庭園公園), once the site of a daimyo mansion. The owner laid out what was recognized then as one of the most beautiful landscape gardens in the city. Today it is still impressive with its ponds and paths and greenery. Baron Yasuda gave the park to the city in 1922. The next year brought the Great Kanto Earthquake, and much of it was destroyed.

Adjacent to the park is a temple site that commemorates the horror of the day and the thousands who lost their lives. At the time of the earthquake, this was a vast, open area, and of course people, bringing along whatever possesions they could carry, sought refuge here. As the flames following the quake engulfed the city, sparks ignited their belongings, and it is estimated that 35,000 people burned to death on this spot: there was nowhere else to go.

Today, in the three-storied pagoda of the Earthquake Memorial Hall (東京都慰霊堂), the charred remains of the victims are kept in large urns, and incense has burned continuously in front of the altar since it was first lighted four days after the tragedy. A memorial service is held every year on September 1. During World War II, the ashes of many victims of the air raids were also brought to the temple to be enshrined in the memorial building.

The museum across the courtyard holds shattered, twisted remains of those disasters—melted bottles, torn and rusted metal, clocks stopped at the moment of disaster—a sad and rather neglected reminder of past horrors.

And it is perhaps time to pause a moment and accept that such tragedies are not relegated to the past, and this area throughout history has always suffered the most when disaster strikes. Even today, the low-lying land, the crowded conditions, and the lack of appropriate shelters or escape routes cause experts to shake their heads in despair over what will happen to the people who live and work alongside the Sumida River when another disaster occurs.

Perhaps it is appropriate that there is a hospital nearby, Doai Kinen Byoin, or the Fraternity Memorial Hospital. It was built with funds contributed by America following the earthquake.

Now Kuramaebashi (蔵前橋), another bridge to cross. Watch for a marker on the right on the other side. Once there were huge warehouses—*kura*—for rice storage here. Tremendous spaces were necessary. The daimyo were paid in rice, and there were dealers who then bought it from the daimyo, paying in the coins these lords needed to meet their own expenses. The complex distribution system of Japan was established at a very early day.

Next, the sprawling Kokugi-kan, (国技館) where Tokyo's sumo tournaments are held three times a year, in January, May, and September. It was built in 1954 and has both seats and boxes (where people sit on cushions on the straw-matted floor), watching the matches while they consume great quantities of tea, beer, *yakitori,* rice balls, and other lunch-box foods, following the great traditions of Edo when eating and entertainment were always best when appreciated together. The building, as mentioned before, is slated for demolition, and no decision has been announced concerning the future use of the site. High rise apartments that overlook the river is one guess.

You can walk inside. At the right of the gate is a small building with a museum on the second floor. The ancient history of sumo is depicted in a sculpture from the Heian period (794–1185), a delightful threesome of sumo wrestlers and referee. Also outstanding is the wide scroll with sumo-san in full regalia awaiting, one supposes, entrance to the ring. Their expressions and postures suggest the humor of today's cartoonist rather than that of a twenty-eight-year-old painter two hundred years ago (as the sign tells us). There is much more to catch the interest of those with even a fleeting interest in the sport. One, an interesting explanation of why the sumo ring is round. In the old days people gathered around the wrestlers in a circle to watch. This interfered with the action, so a circle was outlined with straw barricades filled with earth and stone. The same general form is followed today.

There are *tabi* (Japanese socks) with a sign saying they are so large that each one could hold two *sho* of rice (two *sho* would be more than three quarts.) If you wonder about the top hat and stick, they commemorate the visit to the U.S. of two sumo men in 1915. No photo shows how they dressed, but certainly a *mawashi*, the standard loincloth worn by sumo wrestlers, would have been quite a shock to the staid New Englanders of those days.

You are asked to request permission at the entrance to go inside the hall, and it is usually granted, except of course on tournament days when you need a ticket. The building is put to other uses when the sumo wrestlers are away, such as boxing and Western-style wrestling. Occasionally a children's tournament is held, with all the ceremony of a real match, and all the joys and disappointments of winner and loser. If it is your lucky day, you might be there for a practice session.

Now, back to the main street and the next subway station. You are now at Kuramae (蔵前), and you should linger a while in this well-known wholesale area. This is where people come to buy the decorations that seasonally brighten the streets of Tokyo, the cherry blossoms of spring and the tinted fall leaves (all in gloriously colored plastic) and, in the fall, Christmas ornaments. Each season has its specialty, but, since it is a wholesale area, they occur two to three months before the event.

There are toys too (one shop sells only balloons) and paper products, clothing and—but we will leave you to discover for yourself the variety provided by the wholesalers of Kuramae. You may not find what you set out to look for, but inevitably there will be many other things that you will want, perhaps not even realizing how much you needed them before you walked along the streets of Tokyo's wholesale district.

浅草

Asakusa: Sparse Grass

ASAKUSA! This is Tokyo's greatest showplace, with its old amusement center and its famous Kinryu-san Senso-ji temple. The name translates Golden Dragon Temple of Asakusa, but the Japanese simply call it Senso-ji and foreigners tend to refer to it as the Kannon Temple because it is dedicated to Kannon, Goddess of Mercy, who is especially mindful of the lonely and the destitute.

We make an effort to explain place names, and choose this one to demonstrate how difficult it can be. The characters for *senso* can also be read Asakusa, and both have the same meaning, "sparse grass." *Ji* means "temple." So Senso-ji is also Asakusa Temple.

The word contrasts with the name of an area in Kyoto famous for its thick grass known as Fukakusa, though no one seems to know why it was decided to take note of the difference. There is also the theory that the correct meaning is found in the Ainu language. *Asa kusa* in Ainu means "over the sea," which might answer in part the question of where the Ainu came from. At any rate, there is a record that states "Asakusa" was used for the first time in 1181 to describe this area. Many people who know a few words of Japanese but do not read the kanji assume it means "morning (*asa*) grass," which would seem to be the most image-inspiring meaning of all. Visualize a sunrise, the dew on the morning grass. . . .

And now you know why we don't usually linger long over explaining the meanings of words. But whatever the origin of the name, you are certain to find Asakusa on most tourist itineraries. Here one still finds evidence of Tokyo's plebeian past, a village in the midst of today's prosperous metropolis. In Asakusa, Shitamachi continues to flourish.

We would not have you miss any of it. We will guide you as you jostle your way through throngs of tourists. Most are Japanese. There are country people who find the shops and entertainment in Asakusa far more comprehensible than the designer boutiques, costly restaurants, and expense-account hostess bars in more up-to-date parts of the city. Young people come seeking their roots, the middle aged in search of memories. Geisha, bar girls, and entertainers come, as they have since Edo days, bringing their petitions and problems to Kannon.

We will go through the great Kaminari-mon (Thunder Gate) that marks the entrance to the temple compound, an exact replica of the former gate that was destroyed by the fire bombs of World War II. We will walk along Nakamise, the shop-lined street that leads to the temple. You will marvel at the great variety of merchandise that bridges any gap that exists between Edo and Tokyo. You can buy (again!) bean-paste-filled buns, plastic hair ornaments with cascading chains of flowers and birds, toys, children's geta

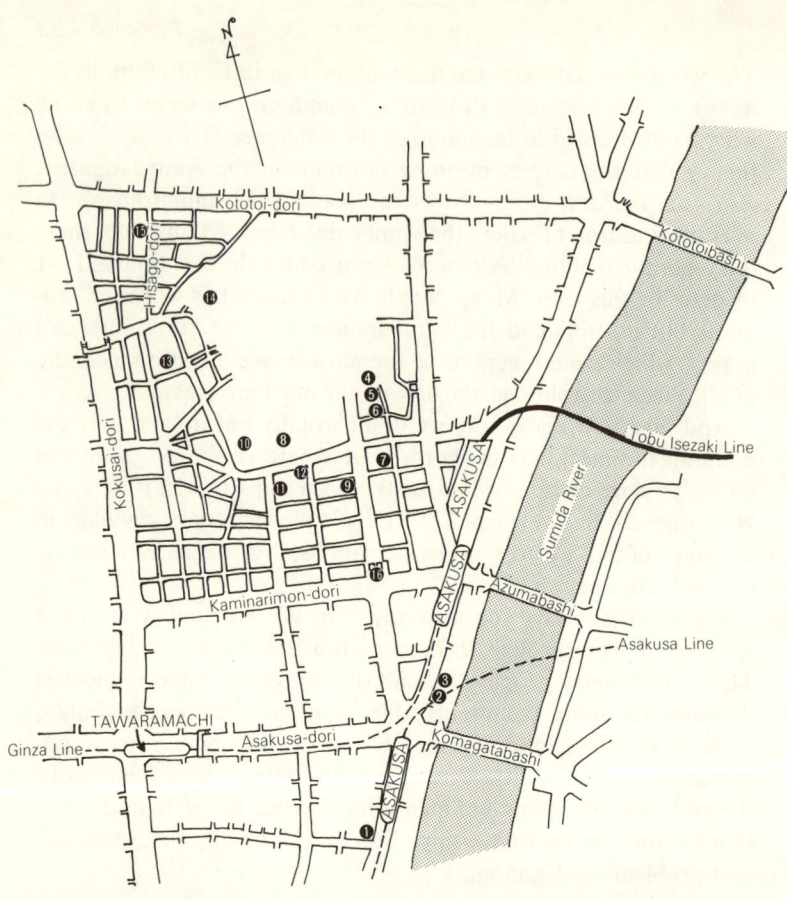

1. Komagata Dojo
2. Mugitoro
3. Miyahara
4. Nakaya
5. Kuremutsu
6. Hyakusuke Shoten
7. Fujiya
8. Dempo-in
9. Umezono
10. Chingodo
11. Taito Ward Kokaido
12. Daikokuya
13. Jogai Baken Uriba
14. Hamayashiki
15. Adachiya
16. Kaminari-mon

that are made to squeak at each step, kimono, happi coats, hairnets, Kabuki stage props, umbrellas, miniatures, and folkcrafts (to only suggest what is offered).

We will tell you, as other guidebooks do, to pause at the giant *koro* (incense burner) in front of the temple and draw the smoke to your body with your hands, just as those around you, young and old, will be doing. For everyone knows the ills of mankind are many and varied, from thinning hair to cancer, from business problems to broken hearts, and the incense is reported to cure them all. Although medical science in Japan is rated among the foremost in the world, such ancient, deep-seated beliefs still exist, comfortably, side by side with science. So, thrust your hand into the smoke, fan it in your direction, and be healed.

We will ask you to admire the giant lanterns that hang from the main hall, each as large as a small house, they say, and to note the huge painting on the ceiling of a dragon escorted by two angels. Legend has it that it appeared miraculously on a day we will tell you about later, when fishermen pulled a golden statue from the sea. It is said that the dragon, the Japanese symbol for fate, lived a thousand years on earth and a thousand in the sea before he returned to heaven in one giant leap, to obtain the jewel which you see in the painting. It represents man's aspirations, and many believe that the dragon has the power to make realities of dreams.

You can still see the dragon itself sometimes in Asakusa. It appears twice a year, in March and October, to dance in the temple courtyard, held high by its handlers who support its writhing golden body on sticks in the Chinese style. The dance is old but the tradition is new. The dragon first danced in 1958 when the new temple, replacing the one destroyed in the war, was dedicated. It was not a new experience. The temple had been destroyed and rebuilt no less than twenty times.

There is another dragon story about the temple. It was said that in the old days, if you looked toward Asakusa from across the Sumida River, the outline of the temple against the sky resembled a great dragon. No one could verify this today: too many tall buildings now obstruct the view.

Although the golden dragon is cherished, in truth the temple belongs to Kannon, Goddess of Mercy. We are told that the tiny golden statue of Kannon that is enshrined in the temple was brought up in the net of three brothers, fishermen, in the year 682. This image of the deity, only two inches tall, was immediately enshrined, and that is when the dragon first appeared. In 635, the first temple to house her was completed, making it the oldest temple dedicated to Kannon in Tokyo. The goddess has never been seen since her enshrinement. As the box that holds her becomes worn, it is encased in another layer of three wooden containers.

Of course there was one exception—isn't there always?—in early Meiji days, when doubters, armed with false documents, demanded to be shown the image. They were, and they were all struck dead soon after under very mysterious circumstances. Since then the goddess has maintained her enforced solitude in a box within boxes. She is a true goddess, unseen, existing on faith alone.

Asakusa is the Japan that all tourists dream of seeking, the woodblock print come to life, the painted teacup a reality. There are many festivals—hardly a month goes by without one: the dance of the golden dragon, the gloriously boistrous Sanja Matsuri, the lantern festival, drawing thousands to Asakusa, contributing to the well-being of both shopkeepers and temple.

To say it was the "heart of the entertainment district" cannot even begin to indicate the Asakusa of old. Nearby was Yoshiwara, Edo's pleasure quarters, and the wealth exchanged there drew the finest craftsmen and artisans to please the people who had the money to reward them for their skills. Artists recorded the life of the area for posterity and poets put words to the pictures. Wealthy merchants built their mansions near where the money was, and while they walked the streets in the prescribed cotton kimono, everyone knew the lining was of the finest silk. (In those days, the shogun government regulated even the type of clothing each class of people could wear; for the merchants, it was cotton.) But not everyone could afford the best, so that was something for everyone regardless of how much or how little he had in his purse.

In Japan, there has always been an affinity between religion and the sensual. Asakusa, with the Kannon Temple and the nearby Yoshiwara, provided both.

There was a theater district where traditional drama flourished. So did Kabuki performed by women, until it was outlawed. Later, after the war, it resurfaced again for a few years, with women playing the parts of both samurai and court lady, adding an element of nonsubtle sexuality not readily apparent in conventional performances.

And more! The postwar years brought new life to the area. It had been leveled by the firebombing of Tokyo but was rapidly rebuilt, with the reconstructed Kannon Temple, paid for by contributions from the people, leading the way. Once again people could bring their petitions to the compassionate Goddess of Mercy. And in the back streets, as in the past, shops sold gaudy souvenirs, and medicines and devices to enhance sensual pleasures. The traditional strip shows (flip open a kimono with a sword, use a folding fan to almost cover what the audience most wants revealed) were augmented by a new style, strip *tease,* a gift, the people said, along with chewing gum, from the West. (See the story of Japan's first strip tease in *Foot-loose in Tokyo,* Shinjuku chapter.)

Samurai dramas were performed on stage, not TV, and people flocked to Asakusa to see the heroines abducted and villains slain, and in those early days, the overwhelming aroma of *daikon* pickles and camellia hair oil could be as odious to the uninitiated foreigner as the gory death scenes on stage.

And the people still come, seeking excitement, titillation. Now there are "pink" films as well. Vivid posters, featuring bright colors and nudes in provocative positions, promise a farrago of sensual fare for the curious, though those who are familiar with Japan's strict standards of censorship know they will see a lot of smudges that effectively mask explicit details, and certainly no pubic hair. It has been outlawed, at least in popular art forms, accounting for an interesting profession for part-time workers, usually male college students or old women, who black out offensive portions of photos in imported publications—at what peril to *their* morals, one wonders.

There are strip theaters too, and touts to attract the customers. It is an easy sell, for the late-night shows provide more than entertainment. They also offer cheap sleeping places for those with nowhere to go.

Asakusa also has live sex shows (some offer private cubicles for viewing, others invite volunteer participation) but they maintain no regular address because of the vigilance of the police.

Traditional Japanese vaudeville, mostly comic storytellers and a few musical or magic numbers, thrive alongside the strip shows and pink movies, pachinko parlors, and game arcades. Asakusa continues to provide amusements for all who seek them.

You are too late for the Kokusai Gekijo, the largest theater in all of Asia, seating more than five thousand people. Here was a stage show that held its own against the best of Las Vegas or Paris reviews. Each show included a spectacular fire scene in which a palace or a castle went up in flames. The last performance, in the spring of 1982, changed the format for the finale. A rocket was launched from the stage, complete with smoke and fiery exhaust, and an astronaut's sweetheart, left behind, shed tears as the rocket disappeared off into the distance among the curtains and the props and the memories.

Scheduled to replace the theater is a new hotel, to be completed in 1985, with twenty-five floors, 430 guest rooms, shops, and offices. It is hoped that it will be a keystone in revitalizing Asakusa. The name, as of this writing, will be Japan View Hotel, which would indicate even broader goals.

There have been efforts before to revitalize Asakusa, but it still holds on to the past. Old people come to catch a glimpse of other days, young people seek their roots in the friendly, plebeian streets of Asakusa, and the curious come to watch, for everyone knows that in Asakusa the gods are more tolerant, the entertainments more earthy, the prices cheaper.

And you should come too, for there is much to see. If you want to arrive in a style from the past, take a water taxi from Takeshiba Pier near Hamamatsucho Station, or from a stop at the Hama Detached Palace Garden (see Shimbashi chapter, *Foot-loose in Tokyo*). Watch for the old geisha houses along the left bank, the first, Jisaku, just past the Tsukiji fish market, looking like a giant temple complex with tile-roofed buildings. In the "taxi" (actually it's more like a bus) one could do without the recorded voice that tells us in what year the bridges were constructed and how much metal went into the project, but that, too, is part of modern-day Japan, where a quiet corner is considered a vacuum and something is hurried in to fill it. On weekends, when tourist traffic is heavier, you may be provided with English explanations of some of the sights along the way, interspaced with more personal observations concerning such topics as the bathing and eating habits of the Japanese.

The boat will drop you off where you want to be, at the entrance to greater Asakusa. But then, so will the subway. Take your choice.

To the right as you leave the boat landing, in the narrow streets that radiate from the temple grounds, one still finds many dealers in shoes, drums, and other leather goods. There was a need for leather in the old days—it was used to lace the plates of samurai armor, for example—but Buddhism did not permit the taking of life (warriors were apparently exempt from this ruling) and Shintoism abhorred death, so a special class of people evolved to deal in the leather trade and to handle executions. Although their work was essential, they were disdained by other Japanese. They lived in special communities and were referred to, not by their derogatory name *eta,* which means "great filth," but as *burakumin,* or "village people." With the Meiji Restoration, the new constitution ended all forms of discrimination, but the story is told that, although the records which identified the village people were burned, copies had been made beforehand, and even today, people of burakumin background suffer when seeking employment or entrance into universities, and marriage plans are often terminated when it is whispered that the proposed partner is "one of those." Today, they are fighting more effectively for their rights.

A good place to begin—though you may just want to slide open the door and look—is one of the area's most famous restaurants, Komagata Dojo,[1] known for mud fish, or *dojo.* While Japanese appear to relish these fish, their popularity may be attributed more to their reputation for ensuring "stamina"—in Japan, that has to do with sexual vigor—than to taste. The method of serving is unique and hardly appetizing. The dojo come to you alive, swimming in a soy sauce broth, and are gently cooked on the table in front of you on a small charcoal stove. But the setting is plesasant, a huge tatami-matted room with the lowest tables in town: they are simply boards on the floor.

Back to the corner, and another restaurant that reflects individual preference. Everything served at Mugitoro[2] contains *yama imo* (a kind of yam), a vegetable with a consistency unfamiliar to Westerners, and generally unappreciated. But the shop is attractive with tea-ceremony umbrellas, folkcrafts for sale, packages of pickles, and of course, yams.

Next door, Miyahara (宮原) sells whatever is needed for traditional engagement and wedding rites. Here you can buy the elaborate envelopes for cash gifts, the auspicious decorations made of

1. Komagata Dojo, 1–7–12 Komagata, Taito-ku; tel. 842–4001
   駒形どぜう　台東区駒形 1-7-12
2. Mugitoro, 2–2–4 Kaminarimon, Taito-ku; tel. 842–1066
   麦とろ　台東区雷門 2-2-4

twisted paper cords, the trays and stands and covers that are required even today when gifts are formally presented. Pricing some of the more elaborate creations, you will discover that the wrappings would cost more than you intended to spend for the gift. But not everything is expensive, and you will probably select a colorful tortoise or crane made of intricately contrived loops of twisted gold-colored paper even if you can't think of a use for it (tie it on a Christmas tree).

Now, do what visitors, Japanese and foreign, all do at Asakusa Kannon Temple (浅草観音): walk along Nakamise to the temple everyone comes to see. Buy some souvenirs, sample the sembei, breathe in the incense, toss a coin in the money box, admire the dragon—and now that you have done everything a good visitor does, continue on the exploration of the less familiar Asakusa.

Instead of repeating your steps, turn left as you leave the temple to the second narrow lane. On the corner is Nakaya,[3] a shop that appears to sell only things for children. But at the back you will discover a fascinating variety of old-style merchandise—festival costumes, cotton purses to be suspended from obi or belt, temporary tattoos (or body-tattoo T-shirts)—a tremendous variety of attractive items that make ideal gifts, though you will want some for yourself as well.

Nearby is a restaurant for those who come late to the temple. In Japan, that means any time after, say, 4 P.M. That's when people start to gather at Kuremutsu,[4] though the name actually means six o'clock in the evening. It is true that some of the shops in Nakamise will stay open as late as nine, but the crowds are sparse at that time of night. Shitamachi goes to bed early. Quite a few of the late-comers will be there because of this old, traditional restaurant, filled with furnishings of the past and serving the characteristic

3. Nakaya, 2–2–12 Asakusa, Taito-ku; tel. 841–7877
   中屋　台東区浅草 2-2-12
4. Kuremutsu, 2–2–13 Asakusa, Taito-ku; tel. 842–0906
   暮六つ　台東区浅草 2-2-13

food specialties for which Japan is famous—as long as they are considered a proper companion for sakè, because the two go together when a person is seeking relaxation at a *sakaya,* the name for this type of restaurant. But even here, you cannot plan on a late night out, for the doors close firmly at ten. The bill? It won't be a bargain, but you wouldn't expect one at a restaurant that introduces you so pleasantly to the fine Japanese art of convivial drinking and dining.

(If it is a bargain you are after, choose to have your evening meal at one of the food stands behind the temple where broths with questionable contents bubble in huge caldrons, as they have for evening diners since Edo days. Here you can buy a bowl of hot Japanese-style stew at perhaps the cheapest price in town.)

A few doors down the street, on the corner, is Hyakusuke Shoten (百助商店), a shop selling old-time cosmetics, hair ornaments, and stage makeup. Now is your chance to try such ancient favorites as dried nightingale droppings. Dissolve in warm water and pat the preparation on your face as Japan's beauties used to do. Of course you can buy this *uguisu no fun* at bird stores too, but the government frowns on such unauthorized sales. Even nightingale droppings should be of the highest quality, and what you buy here, in pink, butterfly-decorated packages, is certified pure.

Or perhaps you would like to buy your lipstick in a lacquer sakè cup. *Benibana,* made from the safflower, is applied with the tip of a finger. No advertisement has ever claimed that it lasts all day: it doesn't. The color fades quickly. Still, no modern lipstick produces that soft green-gold undertone that comes from benibana. There is also a lotion made from cucumbers, another from gourds. Japanese grandmothers used these products, and their vibrant skin tones serve as testimonials to what some might disparagingly call folk remedies.

A little further along is Fujiya (ふじ屋), a shop selling the narrow cotton hand towels called *tenugui* that find so many uses in Japan—for gifts, to wind into a cord to tie around the head (a common adornment of sushi-shop workers), and, of course, towels. You will see their promise as decorator items too. The designs are appealing—a geisha under a willow tree, a Kabuki figure in earth-tone colors, calligraphy. Visualize them framed, used as napkins and table mats, as kitchen towels, and take some home for yourself and for gifts. Each will be folded inside a traditional paper wrapper with a printed-on decoration that means "gift."

You can also order a happi coat or a noren to hang over your doorway with your own name or design. Simply seeing the rolls of sample materials is a pleasure for anyone who appreciates fabrics.

Now, turn left to the main Nakamise and find Umezono,[5] a shop selling the sweet things so loved by Japanese women, the bean-paste confections, the ices, the gelatin-like desserts piled high with chopped ice, whipped cream, and fruit. Try something. It is a tradition of Asakusa, and the shop has been a favorite for years.

As you contemplate what has been set before you, you can consider what other things you would like to see. You must have noticed the towering pagoda. It is modeled after the one at Daigo-ji, a temple in Kyoto which was built in the tenth century. Asakusa's was built in 1973, replacing the former pagoda that was destroyed in the war. It is made of ferroconcrete, and the roof tiles are of aluminum.

Perhaps you will pause to look (over a fence) at Dempo-in temple (伝法院), where the chief abbot of the great Senso-ji, or Kannon Temple, resides; it is one of the few buildings in all of Tokyo that dates back to the Edo period. It has a famous landscape garden designed by Kobori Enshu, one of the masters of the art of gardens and tea ceremony, but few people are given permission to see it.

Would you like to be one of those exceptions? No problem. Walk down to the next corner and turn to the right. Shops, most of

5. Umezono, 1–31 Asakusa, Taito-ku; tel. 841–7580
   梅園　台東区浅草　1-31

them little more than stalls, sell kimono and imitation World War II uniforms. Among them you will find a dealer in abacuses and a comb maker, a fan peddler and a store selling objects made of tortoise shell and coral. Watch on the right for the entrance to Chingodo (鎮護堂). The main gate is often closed but you can go in through a small door on the left. You will think you are in kiddieland, for there, lined up to catch even the most fleeting breeze, are hundreds of twirling pinwheels. You have come to see a garden (and there it is: just look over the fence at the back) but you are also at a temple where people come to pray for the souls of aborted infants. And you will see the mourners—young couples, grandparents-that-might-have-been, families with the brothers and sisters of the children that never were.

Japan early on faced—and dealt with—the problem of overpopulation, and today a Japanese family has an average of 1.8 children. Abortion is an accepted means of birth control in a country that has not yet approved the pill, a decision, you will be told, that was made because it is not yet considered safe (though they are made for export). Some suggest that it is a way of keeping women from falling into the relaxed ways of the West, others accuse doctors of supporting abortion as a profitable part of their profession.

For many families, the reason for abortion is financial; raising and educating more than two children is a tremendous burden. And there are not the cultural barriers to abortion that there are in Christian, and especially Catholic, countries. But few can undergo an abortion without some feeling for the child that will never be born. Consequently, a number of temples have made a specialty of bringing solace to the parents of the child that might have been wanted but was still denied existence. You can recognize these temples by the pinwheels, each marking a memorial to a "lost" baby. As they turn in the breeze, they repeat the message, "I'm sorry." You will also see a lot of offerings for the babies: little hats, and bibs, and folded-paper cranes. Fold a thousand of these and the gods will hear your prayer . . . and perhaps they will bring a special blessing to the spirit of a lost child.

The *tanuki* is the guardian of this temple, and he will hear your prayers, especially if you buy a miniature of this little raccoon-like creature at the shrine office and leave it behind, along with your request. The tanuki is best known for its association with sakè. You will often see its statue in front of a sakaya, sakè bottle in hand, ready to join the party. And it is said that he often does, for he has the ability to assume the shape of a human, perhaps even someone you know. You never can be really sure when a friend joins you for a drink that he isn't a tanuki. If you are left with the bill, chances are it wasn't your friend. Tanuki are skilled at avoiding payment.

A wise tanuki might skip the sakè bar for a lunch invitation at Daikokuya,[6] a famous tempura house across from his temple. It serves an old-style version, with a heavier batter, but it is still light and tender, and you will probably come back for more. Why not? The restaurant claims a hundred years of satisfied customers.

Shortly beyond, at the corner, you will see the Asakusa Kabuki Theater. Now that should bring back memories even if you have never seen a performance. But actually, you have, in all those woodblock prints, the people sitting on tatami mats watching the show, eating their lunches, spending the day at the theater. You may want to pull up your mat and join them.

Well, I'm sorry to say that you are at the wrong theater. Asakusa holds on to its past, but not in this block. Today's Kabuki is held in a rather sterile building following the plan of most city halls, for this is the Taito Ward Kokaido (台東区公会堂). But then, in a way, it is the same, for couldn't today's citizens' hall be a modern interpretation of the place where people gathered in past days? It has rooms for concerts, dramas, and other activities, with Kabuki scheduled several times a year.

6. Daikokuya, 1–38–10 Asakusa, Taito-ku; tel. 844–1111
   大黒家　台東区浅草 1–38–10

Usually, people wanting to see Kabuki will go to the Kabuki-za in the Ginza (near Tsukiji), or seek out the past at the Meiji-za alongside the Sumida River (see Ningyo-cho chapter). They will come to Asakusa for the *rakugo* (storytelling) and the strip theaters and "pink" movies and the temple (which always hears the requests of the common man) and the—

Would you believe, off-track betting? Look over there, at that splendid chrome and red-brick building, strangely deserted or engulfing an endless stream of patrons depending on whether or not it is a race day. It is the Jogai Baken Uriba,[7] where people bet on the horses.

Some countries have laws against off-track betting. Not Japan. The way has been eased to place bets anywhere, and technology has simplified the procedure. If you are a regular bettor, you don't even have to go to the track, or even to the betting center for that matter. You can have your voice recorded, and from then on, chance is as close as the nearest phone, which is on almost any corner in Japan. Just call in your bet and it will be taken by a computer that is programed to recognize your voice and thank you for calling. Then, when the race is over, your bank account will automatically receive a deposit or you will be charged for a withdrawal, depending on whether or not it is your lucky day. Like the ancient samurai who, it is said, disdained money, you never have to touch the stuff. Only your bank knows.

Overseeing the vast empire that covers Japan is the Japan Racing Association under the benevolent gaze of the Minister of Agriculture, Forestry, and Fisheries. The association operates ten race tracks, two training centers, horse-rearing farms, equestrian parks, a school for jockeys, a number of research institutes, and of course the betting facilities. For the convenience of bettors, only one type of ticket is sold on each floor: one thousand yen for the big spen-

7. Jogai Baken Uriba, 2-8-6 Asakusa, Taito-ku; tel. 844-0095
   場外馬券売場　台東区浅草 2-8-6

ders, five hundred yen for the intermediates, and one hundred yen for the small-time bettors, who comprise more than fifty percent of those placing bets.

Women take the bets. "Men tend to buy more from women," an attendant explained, adding that business is always good. "It's a recession-proof enterprise," he emphasized.

The building is utilitarian. No provision is made for comfort. There are no chairs, not even a television set so that patrons can watch the races. The reason: with the tremendous number of people placing bets, it is felt that TV coverage would be a hazard.

So bettors wait in the streets, and a large number of fast-food restaurants are in the vicinity to serve them. But it is not hamburgers or fried chicken they are ordering. It is *soba* and *domburi* and *oden,* all low-priced Japanese specialities that are featured at some of the cheapest prices in town. There are TV sets too, so that bettors can monitor the tracks.

When the races are over and the winners bring in their tickets for collection, they are run through a scanner which provides an automatic printout of the amount won.

(When betting on the horses first began, a winner would slide his hand beneath a black-curtained window to receive his money. This way no one could see how much he had won. Today the system is still used by love hotels but for other reasons. Payment for the room is slipped under a black-curtained window at the reception desk so that the guest cannot be seen by the hotel employee.)

Horse racing is not new to Japan. Emperor Meiji watched horses race around Shinobazu Pond in Ueno as early as 1884, a sport he had perhaps learned from the foreigners who were coming to Japan in increasing numbers. One of the initial projects of early settlers was to establish a racetrack in Yokohama. The first race was held in May 1862.

Horse racing has a much longer history than that, however. There is reference to something that at least resembled a race at a court ceremony in 701, and a race was reportedly held at Kamo

Shrine in Kyoto in 1093. While the shoguns ruled from Edo, members of the emperor's court in Kyoto amused themselves with effete entertainments such as the incense ceremony, where winners were chosen by their ability to guess the name of an exotic incense from only a gentle whiff. One game used a horse-race format, and each correct guess allowed the player to move his horse a few paces forward. You can see these beautifully made miniatures with metal fittings, brocade blankets, and flowing manes at all-too-rare exhibitions when objects associated with incense ceremonies are displayed.

And now, horse racing is being internationalized. The first Japan Cup race was held in 1981. Invitations to the foreign participants included first-class round-trip tickets, hotel accommodations at top hotels, and meals for owners, trainers, and jockeys and their wives, and an all-expenses-paid package for the horses and their grooms. Even the losers were winners; all the horse had to do was finish to receive six thousand dollars. The winner, Mairzy Doates, won a purse that amounted to around $300,000 and received the prize along with her owner, jockey, trainer, and groom, who stood at attention on platforms as the band played a trumpet accolade and the crowds cheered. Just like the Olympics.

Times change rapidly, even in Asakusa. It wasn't many years ago that the area where the betting center stands was a children's playground known as *hanayashiki* (flower house). There was a pond where they could try to catch tadpoles and baby frogs. But that was yesterday. Now civic organizations are devoted to restocking the few ponds that are left with frogs. It is a thankless project. It seems they cannot survive in the present city environment.

Now we would like to introduce Hisago-dori (ひさご通り), another of the shopping streets that surround the temple. On the way you will pass many Korean restaurants. This area has always drawn the Koreans, one of Japan's minority groups, and many of them have traditionally made their living in the back streets of Asakusa. The restaurants are one of their enterprises, and if you favor Korean food, you will find some of the best available along this short street.

There are many shops to tempt you, but our destination now is Adachiya,[8] a favorite with workmen and those searching for authentic *matsuri* (festival) outfits. Let it be stressed that these are not lines carried for tourists. These are for use today. Prices may surprise you. Workers do not stint on their clothing. They are made of fine cotton and woolens. Here you can still buy men's topcoats to fit over kimono in the Meiji style and collarless workman's shirts with traditional pine-needle patterns. It is not difficult to find a place in your own wardrobe for some of the attractive, quality clothes and accessories that you will discover at Adachiya.

It is the temple that has, through the years, drawn this diverse collection of shops, amusements, and—people. Why not walk once more through the temple compound, noting how it changes with the time of day, how it blends both past and present.

And finally, as you leave, notice the new and the old at Thunder Gate, which houses two guardian gods, Nio-sama, where you first entered Nakamise leading to the temple. To the left is a shop selling a collection of folkcrafts, many of which claim their origin in Edo days. To the right is a new businessman's hotel, an efficient replacement for the inns where earlier visitors sought rest and amusement, a striking affirmation of the new Asakusa, testifying to change.

In the old days, this part of town rarely attracted those who were only interested in a good night's sleep.

8. Adachiya, 2–22–12 Asakusa, Taito-ku; tel. 841–4915
   あだちや　台東区浅草 2-22-12

Yoshiwara: Good Luck Fields

IN OUR TRAVELS ABOUT TOKYO, we have often mentioned Yoshiwara, the inspiration for artists and poets who left behind a rich legacy of stories, poems, and legends depicting Japan's "floating world of pleasure." It was, perhaps, the most celebrated licensed quarter ever to exist, and it continues today, as near as the Kabuki stage or the woodblock-print gallery; and the courtesan's glorious silks, along with the lacquerware and porcelains she used, are on display throughout the world at museums where people marvel at their perfection.

The very name by which it was known—the floating world—

marks its pleasures as transient, and this was as true for the reigning beauties of the day as it was for the peasant girl who scrubbed the floors when she wasn't called to serve some less-demanding customer (a category determined, as always, by the amount of money to be spent).

You can still visit Yoshiwara, but you will take your pleasures in a different fashion. Today it is the *toruko*, or Turkish bath, with enhancements the Turks never dreamed of. In another day, if your pockets were full of gold, you could have chosen the favors of an *oiran*, the most skilled of all courtesans, whose services you could buy—if she agreed, which she generally did if the price was right. You would be buying a night of pleasure with a woman graced in the arts of tea ceremony, flower arrangement, and poetry, as well as the provocative art of the pillow, in which she excelled.

You have seen the oiran in woodblock prints, their high coiffeurs laced through with elaborate hair ornaments, dressed in splendid clothing that demanded the careful attention of apprentices—young girls being trained for the profession of entertaining—whenever they took even one delicate, mincing step. There are many stories of men who squandered their wealth and health in pursuit of an oiran's favor, but in the fleeting world of pleasure, the favor was limited to the length of time the money lasted.

There are stories of courtesans who fled penniless with their lovers (and generally suffered the fate of unaccustomed poverty) and others who committed suicide when their favorite protector finally succumbed to financial ruin, or was dragged home by an angry father or brother who could no longer endure the disgrace— or the squandering of the family wealth. But generally, the leading entertainers of the day closed the door gently at the departure of one patron and opened it graciously to the next.

It was from sheer necessity that an official place for prostitution was first established. When Edo was selected as the capital of the Tokugawa shogunate, many came to make their fortunes in the rapidly expanding city. There are a number of ways to make a

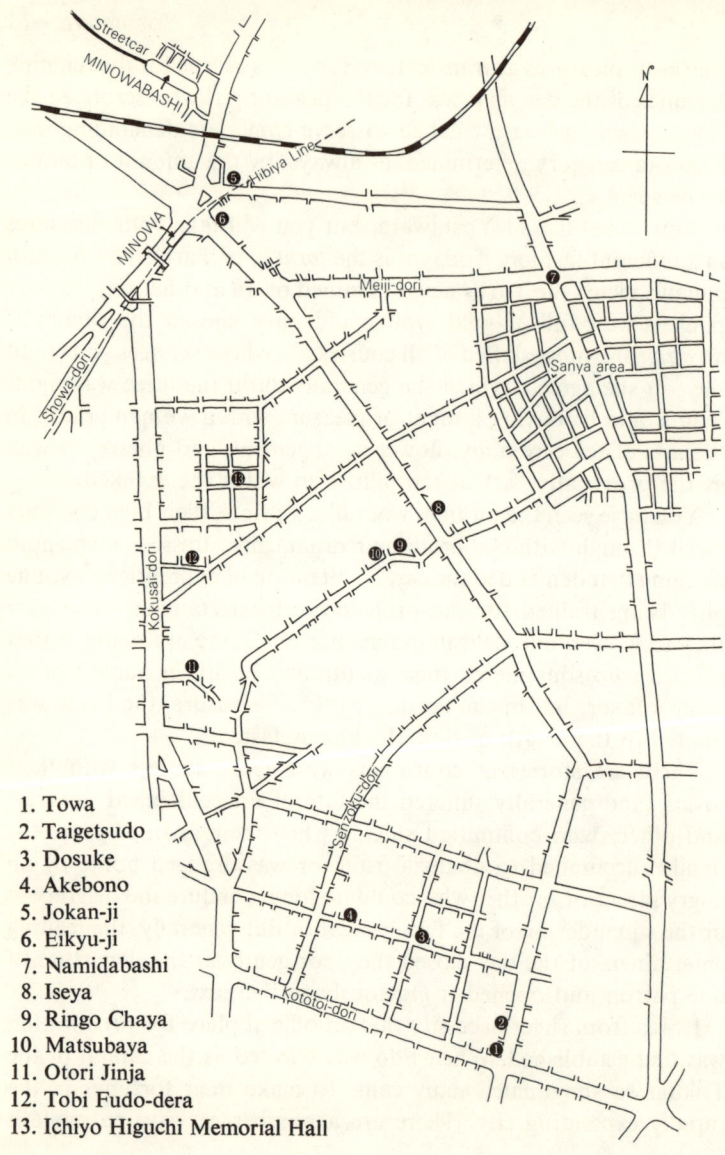

1. Towa
2. Taigetsudo
3. Dosuke
4. Akebono
5. Jokan-ji
6. Eikyu-ji
7. Namidabashi
8. Iseya
9. Ringo Chaya
10. Matsubaya
11. Otori Jinja
12. Tobi Fudo-dera
13. Ichiyo Higuchi Memorial Hall

fortune, and "pleasure women" were a part of the great migration. Still, the number of women compared with men was extremely small. It was not until 1800 that the number of women approached that of men, and even then they were fewer by twenty percent.

In 1617, shortly after Ieyasu had settled in at the Edo castle, he ordered that all the prostitutes be brought together in one place, in an area that is now known as Ningyo-cho. After the big fire that leveled the city in 1657, the quarter was moved to the present location, where it continued to flourish for some three hundred years until prostitution was abolished in 1958.

It is said that an early entrepreneur was responsible for the establishment of an official licensed quarter. Realizing that his business was suffering from amateur competition posed by the women who were arriving in increasing numbers to seek their fortunes in the city, he lobbied for five years to have his plan approved. His points proved appealing to the officials: many people frequented the houses and stayed for days on end in dissipation, forgetting "their station in life and their duties to their masters." If licensed, he pointed out, the government could limit the amount of time spent there, and the money saved could be funneled into taxes paid to the government. In addition, the shogun, fearful of revolt by dissatisfied lords from the provinces, could keep track of those who might be viewed with suspicion by demanding that records be kept of all visitors, thus officially noting the names of those who were in town.

The place was known as Yoshiwara, the same name as that of the previous district near what is now Ningyo-cho. The word may be read as "reed field." It can also be translated as "good luck field." Another explanation of the name is that some thirty of the early residents were from a town called Moto Yoshiwara. Because of their special beauty, or perhaps because of their number, the area took the name of their former place of employment.

There was a gate through which pleasure-seekers passed. Beside the gate was a willow tree where, returning to the real world, one paused to recall the evening's joys. It was known to everyone as "the willow of the backward glance." There is still a willow at the entrance, and people say it is a direct descendent of the original. It is the sort of "people say" that should not be checked too carefully. It is nice to believe that something remains from the past.

These were days of great wealth, with a thriving of the arts and libertine decadence existing contentedly together. Glamorized prostitution had traditionally been supported by officials. With the coming of the wealthy merchant class, money became increasingly important as a determining factor as to who would win the favors of the most popular entertainers. The merchants, who once had been despised as money-grubbers, discovered that within Yoshiwara they were not only the equals of the upper classes, but they could even surpass them in buying pleasure. The samurai, who valued austerity and disdained wealth (perhaps because there was no way for them to amass it), based their power on courage, loyalty, and their swords. These were not a medium of exchange in Yoshiwara.

It took great wealth to even approach an oiran. There are many stories of merchants who demonstrated their prowess through their pockets. One reportedly closed the gates of Yoshiwara for two days, limiting entrance to his friends in defiance of all regulations, which no doubt demanded a number of palms crossed with silver, or *ryo,* the gold coins of the day. In this way, for himself and his friends, he purchased the favors of everyone within the walls of Yoshiwara.

At any one time throughout Yoshiwara's long history, there were probably no more than two or three oiran, but there were talented women of lesser rank available for those who could not always afford the best. Their skills too were renowned. It is said that geisha developed from this group of entertainers.

Although these women were prostitutes, it seems rather inelegant to refer to them in so prosaic a way. Grace and charm were their attributes. They were great beauties, and many a man happily sacrificed his money and his reputation for the pleasure of being in the presence of a favorite.

Emphasis was not only placed on the delicate art of making love. Other attributes were also stressed. Poems were written at picnics, love letters studded with clever ambiguities were slipped into sleeves, and the courtesans knew their classics and could identify incense after but one whiff. Excursions were made into the countryside, and the women took along extra kimono for a change in the afternoon (a harbinger, perhaps, of the multichanges of costume at today's wedding ceremonies). The extra kimono would be hung from a frame, or more rustically, from a branch, ostensibly providing a shelter from the wind, but in actuality, with its colors and design, creating a second landscape against the natural scenery. (Today, the old screens that reproduce these scenes sell for millions of yen.) There were poetry parties, and perhaps the viewing of a sumo match, where all could marvel at the tremendous size of the giant wrestlers. Picnic lunches were arranged in lacquerware boxes, with detailed attention being given to season and color, and sakè was sipped from tiny porcelain cups. For the oiran and their patrons, it was an age of great extravagance.

This was the world of the ukiyo-e, the floating world of transient pleasure, typified by the cherry blossom, which is most beautiful just before it fades, and the maple leaf, unexceptional until it bursts into color, its glory a prelude to its fall. Love affairs and money were life's main pursuits. One did not fight with life, one drifted with its current, living for the moment, like a gourd floating downstream. Tomorrow was always a nighttime away, and today's pleasures were yet to be counted.

In Yoshiwara, those who ranked at the top of their profession entertained in houses that defied the regulations prescribing austerity of decoration. Walls and ceilings were painted by the famous artists of the day, a riot of color accentuated by gold and silver leaf. Fittings were of *maki-e,* a kind of gold-decorated lacquer. Kimono were embroidered with threads of gold and silver, and no one in the world has ever matched the skill of the dyers of those days who created fantasies in design which accentuated the season. Even undergarments were lavishly decorated, and quilts were crisscrossed with threads of gold and silver. Extravagance was a way of life, and for a country that at least officially placed virtue in austerity, the contrast was devastating. It is no wonder that the oiran were also known by another name: *keisei,* or a beautiful woman who brings her lord's castle to ruin.

One visitor describes the scene: houses are lit by lanterns which barely reveal the women in gorgeous kimono kneeling properly behind the latticed windows in front of delicately painted Japanese screens. Occasionally, one responds to a summons and rises gracefully to greet her lord for the evening. The haunting sounds of samisen fill the air, and passers-by can hear the tabi-clad feet on the tatami matting as the steps of classic dances are performed. There are gentle laughter and languid sighs. . . .

Among the stories often told of Yoshiwara in song, drama, and dance are those of filial devotion or scandalous deception. The heroine was either sold into the profession in willing acceptance of whatever was required to support her poor and aged parents, or was the innocent victim of a man she trusted who, despite her piteous protestations, sold her for his own profit. Most modern versions have her leaving her "life of shame" for marriage to a tender and loving protector (with at least her heart still pure) to live, one assumes, happily ever after. It has been a popular story on the stage and in novels, but there is little evidence to indicate that in real life there were many such happy endings. A more common conclusion was to be thrown out when one's usefulness was over. You will read later of the temple where these discarded women were cared for until death released them from their sorrow-filled life.

It is true, however, that many of the admirers did buy up the contract of their favorite to establish her in a home of her own in a respectable neighborhood. This way proved to be more reliable and more reasonable than bidding for favors in Yoshiwara. For the age of unprecedented spending was drawing to a close. The lavish squandering of money was being discredited, preceded, perhaps, by a more efficient tax system which may have curtailed expense-account deductions.

When the houses began to feel the pinch, proprietors began exploiting the women. In 1844 an inmate of one of the most famous houses died of what proved to be malnutrition. The others took their revenge by burning down the house, a crime then punishable by death. Yet they were pardoned when the deplorable conditions under which they lived were disclosed. A few years later, after the Meiji Restoration in 1868 that marked the end of the feudal period, newspapers publicized the story of a girl who escaped from her enforced work in the district. The wretched life she had been forced to live caused a wave of indignation to sweep the country, and groups were organized to restore the inmates of Yoshiwara to a more wholesome life.

The abrupt termination of decadent Edo and the creation of a forward-looking Tokyo brought many changes to Japan, and it is not surprising that the new thinking was felt in Yoshiwara as well. The merchant class no longer needed Yoshiwara to provide an escapist's world of pleasure palaces and dreams. Now money was admired, not disdained, and those who had wealth did not need to hide it in the austere clime created by samurai virtues. Instead, exquisite *ryotei*—the word has been translated "geisha houses"—where geisha entertained emerged near the centers for business, industry, and politics. The new leaders no longer needed to seek their pleasures in Yoshiwara.

The houses remained, but there was less subtlety. Now the women's photographs were displayed alongside the door, and a customer would pause at the ticket office to pay his fee. The women still smiled and beckoned from behind the wooden-slatted windows that foreigners, unfamiliar with Japanese architecture, described as "cages." The same services were provided but the system was vastly different from the days when arrangements were discussed over teacups and conversation, when resorting to a quotation from an old Chinese poem to mask a direct question could be part of the game.

Then, in the spring of 1945, the district, and all that was left of Yoshiwara's former glories—the occasional building that maintained a few vestiges of better days—disappeared as the firebombs rained down on Tokyo.

Gradually, it was rebuilt. There was a need for such places for comfort after the humiliating defeat, and while it was "off limits" to occupation forces, some of these men, too, inevitably found their way to the doorways of the district's houses, now built on a far simpler scale, though there could be no doubt of the business conducted within.

What was thought to be the final blow to Yoshiwara came in 1958, when the antiprostitution law was passed. The date was April 1, but the law was no April Fools' Day joke, although one newspaper, taking note of the long debate that had preceded the final action, reported that the end was caused by acute legislation. Many of the houses were boarded up, and the women who had worked there were sent off to rehabilitation centers.

But Yoshiwara seems fated to exist, having overcome countless disasters in the past. Gradually the doors reopened, gaudy neon lights replaced the lanterns, and the Japanese institute of the Turkish bath—toruko—emerged to bring new prosperity to the area, and the Turkish-bath girls, with soapsuds and massage and "special services," continue the traditions of Yoshiwara.

There are many approaches to Yoshiwara today, though Edo patrons had only one. Since it was a controlled area, they entered through the main gate. There was a bridge to cross then, but the river that marked the boundary disappeared long ago. Now all that is left is the marker and the lantern and the willow tree, placed there to commemorate the past. The small display is almost unnoticed beside the busy street and is dwarfed by the service station behind it.

If you start out for Yoshiwara from the Asakusa Kannon

Temple, you can be assured of a pleasing walk. Go out the back exit to the right of the main building. Cross the street and to the left you will see Towa,[1] a wholesale outlet for bamboo crafts. Shelves are filled with decorative and utilitarian pieces that well demonstrate why bamboo's popularity endures. It can be formed into so many attractive and useful items. Prices range from a few hundred yen to a million or more, but even the cheapest points up the beauty of the material.

Continuing to walk away from the temple, you will soon pass a shop with attractive woodblock-printed envelopes and folders.[2] The designs are the symbols for various geisha houses. They will be used to hold small gifts, the envelopes for money, the folders to slip over tenugui, the small hand-towel that so often becomes a present given for some courtesy. For more than fifty years Taigetsudo has been printing the delicate designs that mark them for use by geisha.

Next door is a doll shop and, a bit farther on, the attractive shoji-like door marks the entrance to the home of a teacher of samisen and dance. And across the street, in a small, faded building, you may catch a glimpse of the proprietor of an old neighborhood business. Once he ran a profitable agency; he dispatched the jinrikisha that carried the geisha to and from their assignments.

Turn left at a narrow street after the next signal—you will see a tall smokestack that marks a neighborhood sento, or public bath. As you walk along, you will notice occasional houses with distinctive entranceways. Many geisha once lived in this area, and these were their houses.

Watch on the left for the corner workshop of Hideo Suzuki,[3] a coppersmith whose work decorates many temples and shrines.

1. Towa, 3–4–1 Asakusa, Taito-ku; tel. 876–4720
   東和　台東区浅草 3-4-1
2. Taigetsudo, 3–24–9 Asakusa, Taito-ku; tel. 874–3414
   待月堂　台東区浅草 3-24-9
3. Dosuke, 4–9–3 Asakusa, Taito-ku; tel. 874–4715
   銅助　台東区浅草 4-9-3

There are few craftsmen today who can, for example, shape the copper over the wooden forms to make decorative endpieces for their sweeping roofs. His work has been cited by the government, and he has more general recognition as well, for he has appeared on several TV programs.

If you turn to the right and walk down a few doors, you will likely see one of the *o-mikoshi* carried during one of Tokyo's most famous festivals, the Sanja Matsuri held in May. It is an ideal time to study one of these portable shrines. During festival times, the throngs of people and the enthusiasm of the bearers make it impossible to get more than a quick glimpse.

Continue on the same little lane till you spot another chimney, another bathhouse. You will be at the back. If you would like to try a Japanese public bath, this could be your place. Men to the left, women to the right, and remember to wash and rinse before entering the large tub filled with steaming water. We suggest Akebono-yu[4] because of its architectural style—high rounded ceilings laced with old-style latticework in dark wood—and because of the friendliness of the Shitamachi people. Perhaps you have seen the woodblock prints of women in the bath. Akebono-yu will remind you of those prints.

But it is time to move on to Yoshiwara. Turn right after crossing busy Senzoku-dori shopping street (千束通り) and window-shop your way to the willow tree that marks the entrance.

Or, you might choose a different route. Take the streetcar that runs from Waseda to the end of the line, Minowabashi (三ノ輪橋). Arcades filled with stalls and shops would make you think this was once a destination of great importance. And perhaps it still is, but for other reasons. When I was there, a TV crew was filming the arrival of a streetcar, one of the last reminders of old Tokyo. Take a ride before this one, too, disappears.

---

4. Akebono-yu, 4–17 Asakusa, Taito-ku; tel. 873–6750
   あけぼの湯　台東区浅草 4-17

If you come by subway, get off at Minowa Station on the Hibiya Line. Climbing the steps, there is the fleeting hope that this time you will emerge into old Japan, but once again it is a crowded intersection, lined with modern buildings, fogged with truck exhaust.

But it is a quiet place you have come to see—Jokan-ji (淨閑寺), known as Nagekomi Temple. The word *nagekomi* means "thrown in," and it was here where many of the women who worked in Yoshiwara were literally thrown in to die when they could no longer work. There is a large monument to them behind the temple. If you linger there a while, you will surely see someone pause to say a prayer for their peaceful rest. As we added ours, we noticed a butterfly hovering over the tomb. The butterfly symbolizes women who go easily from man to man. This butterfly, quite appropriately, was black, the color of sorrow.

"We must be grateful to these women," a Japanese friend explained. "Because of them, and others like them today, our lives are safer. They take care of that side of men's nature and this protects other women." She paused, and then added, "There were 'comfort girls' in the war. They were sent to the front to take care of the men who were fighting for their country. They didn't want to go but it was their duty. In a way, they went for all of us, and we appreciate their sacrifice. That's why many women come here to burn incense and leave flowers. The world is more comfortable for us because of what they did. They could not help it. Conditions forced them to do what was necessary, and they endured."

The modern marker in front of the memorial is dedicated to the novelist Kafu Nagai, who spent his time in this old part of Tokyo. It provided the setting for his stories about the strippers and prostitutes he came to know. One of his writing brushes and his false teeth are entombed there. He lived in apparent poverty among the poor, but it was discovered after his death that he had accumulated quite a fortune. Perhaps it helped pay for his extravagant monument. He claims a spacious place in the overcrowded temple grounds.

Next, another destination that marks a sad departure. On the way you will pass the temple Eikyu-ji (永久寺) where Meki, a yellow-eyed Fudo, is enshrined. There are several other Fudo deities in Tokyo named for the color of their eyes. This one is in the building to the left of the main temple, barely visible in the darkness. A few doors past the Fudo temple is a shop where tabi and work shirts are made to order.

Perhaps you will choose to skip the next historic spot. Namida-bashi (泪橋) is now a wide and crowded intersection, and there is no evidence of the "bridge of tears" for which it is named. This was the last bridge that condemned prisoners crossed on their way to the execution grounds. For them, there was no hope. There would be no return.

Now the busy corner marks a more modern bridge of tears, for a right turn would take you to Sanya (山谷). Here are today's day laborers, misfits, and vagrants, living in flophouses, or sleeping on street corners with perhaps only a ragged blanket or an old newspaper for comfort. Cheap rice wine or *shochu* is their solace, and the oblivion they achieve sinks them deeper into the mire beneath their own bridge of tears.

It's not a long walk on to Yoshiwara (吉原), or you can go by taxi. If it is lunch or dinner time, look across the street from the entrance for several buildings that wear a look of the past. We suggest Iseya,[5] a tempura house which has been serving satisfied customers since the seventh year of Meiji (1874). You can recognize it by the etched-glass pictures of shrimp that decorate the windows.

Two of the restaurants feature horse meat; both *sashimi* (thinly sliced raw meat) and *sakura nabe,* a hot stew, are especially popular. On down the street is a butcher shop that sells horse meat. You

---

5. Iseya, 1–9 Nihonzutsumi, Taito-ku; tel. 872–4886
　伊勢屋　台東区日本堤 1-9

will notice the bottles of oil displayed in the case. It is obtained from horse fat and is good for burns and fever and, it is said, is especially effective in curing pneumonia.

Horse meat joins a long list of foods and medicines that are reputed to provide stamina, so the restaurants at the gate were frequented by men planning an evening in Yoshiwara. But they were no less popular with those who were leaving, for the meat was also reputed to draw out any poisons that might have entered the body, thus performing a double service. The restaurants continue to prosper.

Go as far as the corner and you will see another covered market area. By now you have traveled through many covered arcades, but this one, free from the influence of curious tourists, may have more of the old-town flavor.

Now, finally, pass the willow tree and enter the main street of Yoshiwara. On the right is a coffee shop Ringo Chaya (リンゴ茶屋), if you would like to contemplate what you have seen—or rest your weary feet. There will be no doubt that the shop once sold antiques. What is left is the owner's private collection.

The street changes with the hour. During the day, it is a rather dingy area with nothing special to mark it. Around 4 P.M., the taxis start arriving, and when the lights come on, it appears even festive. Many of the buildings are constructed in Edo style; the narrow cross streets, if you could erase the purple neon, could be a set for a samurai drama. The image fades when you look at the entranceways of these "Turkish" bathhouses. There are crystal chandeliers, huge arrangements of artificial flowers, and thick lavender or pink carpets.

Where, you might wonder, are the women. None are in sight. But there are several men in front of each establishment, often dressed in tuxedos, and inside are more men, one frequently on his knees, waiting to welcome guests—and to make certain that they understand the charges for the various services which extend the fee well beyond the minimum advertised outside. They don't want any trouble, and here, who would it be who would call for help from the police box on the corner? Prostitution, as we have said, is illegal, and few of the guests would want their names recorded by the police as someone causing trouble in a *toruko*. So it is best to have an agreement in advance.

That is how things are. If you want to see how they were, attend one of the evening shows at Matsubaya,[6] a modern replica of the old Yoshiwara. Here an oiran, the top rank for courtesans, arrives on stage with her attendants and, selecting a guest from the audience, serves him sakè and lights a long, old-style pipe for him, and that's about all. But you can admire her lavish costume and elaborate hair style, and wonder how she can walk on such high geta. There are also songs and dances on the program. You can go alone, with your friends, or join a Tokyo night-life tour. Today's Matsubaya is a restaurant, and dinner guests can either attend the public show or arrange to have a private one in their room—or both.

If you go during the early evening, you will notice a long line of carts alongside Matsubaya, and a few men waiting for evening. They are dealers in oden, a stew made of tofu, turnips, and a variety of fish-paste creations. And *konnyaku,* made from a root vegetable, a gelatinous food that is filling and good for the body, but contains no calories. After dark, the carts fan out to assigned positions, for oden is a popular late-hour refreshment.

There is also a business hotel in the heart of Yoshiwara, for many stay too long and can't get home to their apartments in distant Chiba or Saitama.

Continue along the main street, past the police box, where people may ask for directions but few request help, and out what would seem to be the back door. There was no back exit in the old days. It was arranged so that no one could go in or leave without being observed.

6. Matsubaya, 4–33–1 Senzoku, Taito-ku; tel. 874–9401
   松葉屋　台東区千束 4-33-1

Otori Jinja (鷲神社) is a shrine dedicated to the cock, one of the twleve animals of the zodiac. Each month has at least two cock days and the ones in November are assigned special importance. Then bamboo rakes, known as *kumade* (bear paws), are put on sale. A kumade will bring you great good fortune, for with its assistance, you can rake in good luck, wealth, and even a promotion at the office.

You can go any time of day, but if you buy your rake just after midnight when the cock day is just beginning, you are sure to be especially lucky. Don't pay the first price that is quoted, however. Luck increases with the success of your bargaining. Some of the kumade are elaborately decorated with good-luck symbols, and even the most successful bargainers pay high prices to take one of these home.

Since a cock day comes around every twelve days, there are occasionally three cock days in November. In those years it is said that there will be many fires, and people are urged to be especially careful lest the "flowers of Edo"—the flames that have so often destroyed the city—bloom again.

Unless you go at festival time, however, this famous shrine has little to offer. Built of concrete, embellished with garish and expensive-looking decorations, it seems ideally fitted to be a city shrine. Still, people remember the past, and in spite of concrete courtyards and walks and buildings contrived to look old but certainly are not, the people, those who live in Shitamachi, come regularly to ask for the blessings of the gods.

And well they should, for the shrine has powers well beyond those that have already been listed. All year long it is a pilgrimage stop for a mini-tour of sacred spots dedicated to the seven lucky gods. You will often see them pictured, especially at New Year's time, when, if you are lucky, they will come sailing into your dreams in a boat filled with treasure. You can start your pilgrimage here. For extra measure, there are nine, not seven, shrines on the tour, a rather confusing overlapping, but each god is represented at least once. You can buy a paper at the shrine office and have it stamped at each stop on the route, a souvenir that will assure good fortune. Or so it is said.

How long does it take? The question prompted some debate, but the general consensus was that you should allow about two hours, depending on how long you paused to pray. It didn't seem to make much difference whether you walked or took a taxi. The streets are congested, and some days it's faster on foot.

There are many pilgrimage routes in Japan. There are the thirty-four temples of Chichibu, the expansive national-park area northwest of Tokyo, whose inner sanctuaries are open only one year out of twelve, in the year of the horse. Shikoku has its famous route of eighty-eight shrines. But here in Tokyo, you can make your pilgrimage in only a few hours, an appropriate arrangement because everyone knows how busy people are in the capital, even when it was known as Edo.

The pilgrimages are lucky for the shrines as well. Those who make the rounds toss a few coins in each money box to assure that the gods will hear their prayers, and pay to have a stamp put on the memorial paper that will testify to the completion of the rounds.

It seems true that every shrine or temple must have a gimmick these days if it is to attract the public; incense and candles are not enough. Our next stop, Leaping Fudo Temple or Tobi Fudo-dera (飛不動寺), bases its fame on a legend concerning the Fudo deity that is enshrined there. It seems that a long time ago, perhaps 450 years or so, one of the priests, for a reason that remains obscure, carried the Fudo statue on his back to the top of a mountain near Nara. Here again, the account is not too clear, but it seems the deity felt that he was needed in Edo, and he returned to his temple in one giant leap. For some reason, that seemed to qualify him as a healer of stomachaches.

It took a forward-looking priest to capitalize on the old story. Considering the god's remarkable feat, it's a wonder no one ever thought of it before. Now the flying god offers protection for travelers, with or without stomachaches. It doesn't matter how they go, though he appears to be partial to those who travel by air. His blessing extends over automobiles and airplanes, and even hikers along the road, as is demonstrated by one of the *mamori* (amulets) that you can buy at the temple office. It is a minute pair of *waraji* (straw sandals) attached to a cord along with a tiny bell. Another version has an airplane instead of sandals, and there are other styles as well. Perhaps one of these would make an appropriate gift for your friends who seem always to be leaving on another trip.

There is one more stop you can make before you say goodbye to Yoshiwara, though your sentiments when you leave may be quite different from the reputed sadness of those who paused beneath the willow tree to bid a lingering farewell, at least for a while, to the floating world of pleasure. This is a museum that preserves the manuscripts and personal possessions of a famous writer of Meiji times, Ichiyo Higuchi.[7] If this does not sound very interesting, you may reconsider when you learn that Ichiyo Higuchi was a woman.

Higuchi came from a poor family and had no schooling after the age of twelve. She died of tuberculosis when she was twenty-four. In between, she wrote some twenty novels and many short stories.

It is said that she might have married, but the engagement was broken by her fiance's family when her father died, and her family, already poor, sank into poverty. Higuchi worked at various jobs, among them managing a small shop that sold sweets. One of her novels, set at such a sweet shop, is typical of her works. The romantic stories she wrote were all set in Shitamachi, the neighborhood she knew so well.

Although she had no more schooling—she had stood at the top of her class—she studied writing under a competent teacher, the

---

7. Ichiyo Higuchi Memorial Hall, 3–18–4 Ryusen, Taito-ku; tel. 874–0004
一葉記念館　台東区竜泉 3-18-4

novel-editor of the *Asahi Shimbun,* still one of Japan's leading newspapers. In time the teacher became the lover. While this may have helped further her career, her ability as a writer cannot be denied, and her books are still widely read today. This was quite an achievement for a poor, uneducated woman in Meiji Japan—or anywhere.

At the museum, you will see a model of Yoshiwara's main street, with jinrikisha men waiting for their customers. There is also a replica of her house, which would seem to have provided more room than today's apato do for far wealthier tenants. There are articles of clothing and a few personal possessions, and of course her manuscripts. Even a person with little knowledge of calligraphy will realize her skill as a writer included brush writing as well as composition.

There is also a model of Ogyo no Matsu, the pine tree you have read about in the Negishi chapter. Ichiyo's house was not far from where the tree grew. It too has a place in her novels.

Perhaps, now, you would like to walk back through the streets of today's Yoshiwara. If it is evening, the lights will be coming on and the streets will take on an almost romantic hue. The nighttime shadows are kind to the ersatz plastic and the people in search of profits and transient pleasures. A few of the toruko—Miuraya (三浦屋) and Kadoebi (角海老) for example—still have the same names and locations as in the more illustrious Edo days, but they are far different from the pleasure palaces they imitate. But it is as inevitable that times and techniques will change as it is that there will always be a Yoshiwara somewhere, for everyone who seeks its doorways.

Kappabashi: Raincloak Bridge

KAPPABASHI SELLS kitchenware and restaurant equipment.

Don't let that discourage you. Traditional Japanese kitchenware reflects many of the characteristics of Japanese art: it is simple in form, sparse in detail, appealing to the eye, and perfectly suited to the job it is designed to do.

Of course (because nowhere is perfect) you will also find a lot of garish plastic—dinner plates, kitchen tools, and artificial flowers—but these cannot be considered traditional, and Kappabashi does hold something for everyone. Shopkeepers sell a lot of plastic flowers.

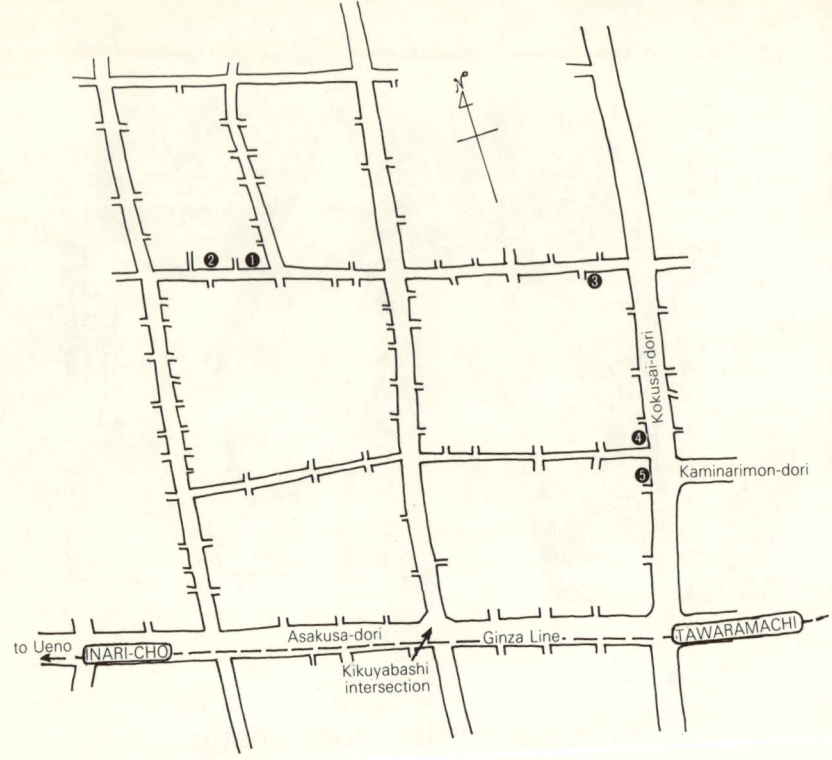

1. Fukuzen-do
2. Sogen-ji
3. Asakusa Kogei-kan
4. Miyamoto Taiko
5. Mitoya

"You can't miss it." How many times have you heard that, and found that indeed it could be missed; in fact it could not be found. But you *can* find Kappabashi. It has a magnificent identification mark. Exit from Tawaramachi Station on the Ginza Line and walk toward the Kikuyabashi intersection (菊屋橋交差点).

Soon you will see it, on top of a building; a gigantic head topped with a chef's hat. And *that* is the beginning of Kappabashi.

Plates, glasses, pans, plastic flowers, baskets, pots, bottles, aprons, name tags, knives, menu covers, chopsticks, signs, copper kettles, cake decorators, strainers, uniforms, bamboo mats, cutting boards—you will see all these before you have passed half a dozen stores. The street stretches on for several blocks, another of those areas where you turn the corner and the present becomes the past. Small, crowded shops line both sides, their wares spilling out onto the sidewalk. Store owners call out to prospective customers, urging them to stop and inspect the splendid merchandise that is being offered—and at such bargain prices!

But what is it for, you may wonder as you see a small, square three-spouted ladle on a long handle. The man who broils eel knows, and he comes to Kappabashi to buy the precise tool he needs to marinate this specialty as it cooks over a charcoal fire.

Then there are *yaki-in,* miniature branding irons that can imprint pictures of cherry blossoms or family crests, or Japanese characters that mean "congratulations" or "the best." Most are about the size of a postage stamp, but there are other, larger ones with scenes of samurai in battle dress or a geisha standing on a willow-shaded bridge with Mount Fuji in the background.

They are put to many uses. A Japanese inn will use its specially designed yaki-in to mark its name on *geta,* the wooden clogs worn by guests when they stroll about the town in the evening, or on the handles of *bangasa,* the oiled paper umbrellas that are available in the lobby for rainy days. Should a careless guest leave his umbrella behind in some shop or sakè-drinking place, someone will bring it back to the inn. (They still do that sort of thing in Japan.) Certain kinds of Japanese sweets and sembei rice crackers are also branded. These show a famous scenic spot or a historic happening. They are sold as souvenirs.

If you have time, you can have one made to order, perhaps with your own name in Japanese.

There are lanterns, ceilings hung with them, some plastic to withstand the weather, a necessary precaution if they are to hang in front of a shop. (Some proprietors, preferring to maintain tradition, still order the more expensive paper ones; then, to protect them, they often wrap them in plastic.) You can order your own, in either plastic or paper, and have it decorated with your name or design. According to the season, you can also find them in the shape of Christmas trees or jack-o'-lanterns, because tradition must keep pace with the times.

Then there are noren, the short, divided curtains, usually made of blue and white cotton, that hang over the entrance of many Japanese shops. In the old days, they served as doors, marking the dividing line between outside and in. They were decorated with the shop's name or mark, and in time they came to symbolize the shopkeeper's reputation. The right to hang a noren identifying a famous shop was passed down from generation to generation, or bestowed on a faithful employee who opened a shop of his own. It was not only an honor to be allowed to use a master's noren, but it also indicated the apprentice's indebtedness to his master as well as the bond that continued to unite them.

Today, a noren shows that a shop is open for business; they are always taken inside when the shop is closed. They are not hung, as some have suggested, for those who want to wipe the dirt from their hands before entering.

Now anyone can hang a noren. As with lanterns, you can have them made to your own design or select one from the wide variety displayed. Some are made of many lengths of thin ropes, often hanging down a meter or so over the doorway. You will see these often at sushi shops, where they are reputed to give a pleasant feeling to those who pass through them. Others may be of wooden beads, strings of bamboo, or today, plastic. It does not take much imagination to adapt them to your own decorating.

Kappabashi is where restaurant owners come to have models made of the foods they serve. These will be displayed in their windows to simplify ordering. They are favorites of imaginative tourists and other shoppers who visualize all sorts of amusing uses for them, as gifts or as "surprises" for their guests.

The models are now made of plastic, though only a few years ago wax was used. It is a demanding art form, and the people who make them are masters of their trade, and their creations look, literally, good enough to eat. Although stock models are on display, most restaurant owners will bring along a sample of the actual foods they serve and the plates, bowls, and dishes they serve them on, for an exact replica. And that is precisely what you will receive when you order from the visual menu, down to the last green pea that decorates the top of your oyaku domburi, or whatever it was you ordered.

The cheapest food model is a single cherry; the most expensive, an elaborate wedding cake. These are used at many wedding banquets. Only one small part of the top layer, the place that is ceremoniously cut by the bridal couple, is real cake. Then the rest is taken away, presumably to be cut, but what is actually served will be from a simpler, edible version.

If you still can't think what you might do with a plastic food model, remember what Andy Warhol did for the tomato-soup can and let your imagination run wild. Whether you put a bowl of imitation noodles topped with plastic shrimp in a shadow box or do a still-life sushi arrangement, the result will be certain to prompt comments. And surely you can think of someone who would appreciate a cup of coffee with a minute cream pitcher suspended above it by a stream of cream, or a plate of spaghetti and meat sauce with the fork held high above it by the pasta to which it is attached.

By this time, you will probably be so hungry (after looking at all these beautifully created foods) that you will be wondering where the restaurants are that serve them, but with few exceptions, it is apparent that although cooks and restaurant owners are Kappabashi's best customers, few are engaged in business there.

There are, however, huge pots for cooking rice; counters, tables, and chairs for the customers; advertising signs for out front; show cases, ovens, and tea roasters; and such surprises as a full-sized wooden Indian or a knight in armor, enhancements for some coffee-shop entrance.

You will also find shops where you can buy ribbon and paper, wholesale, to wrap your gifts. Some bear the designs of famous department stores. Where the gift is from is often as important as the gift itself, and the paper assures credibility.

And, because it somehow seems to stand for what's happening to our world, I would like to point out that you can even buy plastic parsley. The shop owner explained that it didn't matter whether it was real or not because no one ever ate it anyway. As long as it was only a decoration, why should it be edible as well?

You can continue to explore the Kappabashi area, wandering down the cross streets to discover other treasures (whatever they might be) and probably buying them anyway, even not knowing their use, because they are so appealing, and reasonable, and who cares what you are supposed to do with them?

Watch on the right for a corner with a coffee shop, Union (ユ ニオンコーヒー)—but no coffee is served. Instead it supplies everything you could possibly want if you are involved in the serving of coffee, such as brown sugar crystals (bulk sales), coffee cups, sugar bowls, cream pitchers of every size and shape, and an endless collection of accessories for the coffee trade.

This is the Kappabashi intersection (合羽橋交差点). Turn to the left. As you walk along, notice that here, away from foods sealed in plastic and other goods in bubble packs, you can actually *smell* things. There is a maker of tatami mats on the right side of the street, and the scent of the fresh *igusa,* the rush from which the tops of the mats are woven, is a pleasant one. Somewhere there is a bakery and a flower shop. Fish and *miso* blend their aromas, though they may not be your favorites, and occasionally there is a whiff of incense. Remember the old incense games where players tried to identify the scent? You can test yourself as you walk along Shitamachi streets.

Farther along on the right is the workshop of Yasuyuki Sakai, a master sign maker.[1] You will see impressive samples of his work in the windows. He will make a small wooden plaque for your door for a few thousand yen, or a gigantic masterpiece to hang above the entranceway to a temple. Such massive works can take a year to complete.

You will pass two temples before you reach our next destination. Watch for a barber pole and a weathered brown gate. You have found Kappa-dera, or Sogen-ji (曹源寺), the temple for which the area is named. And of course there is a story . . . .

Once there was a narrow canal here, though it has long since disappeared. But in those early days, everyone was very much aware of it. Whenever it rained, the neighborhood was flooded, and finally one of the craftsmen, a maker of *kappa,* the oiled-paper raincoats worn by farmers, decided to build a bridge, which he did. The word for bridge is *hashi.* So, put them together and you get Kappabashi.

That isn't much of a story, but it has been embellished. You see, the word *kappa* has another meaning, and the kappa from the Sumida River came to help with the project. Kappa, as you surely know, could be playful, mischievous or downright dangerous water-sprites depending on whether they were assisting disoriented travelers, tugging at ladies skirts, or pulling unwary children into the water where, sadly, they usually drowned. (One suspects that for years mothers used this tale to frighten children away from dangerous river banks.)

Kappa, about the size of four- or five-year-old boys, are amphibious creatures that inhabit muddy lakes and rivers. From their depictions—and many have been passed down since ancient days—

1. Fukuzen-do, 3–4–1 Matsugaya, Taito-ku; tel. 841–5801
   福善堂看板店　台東区松が谷 3-4-1

they rather resemble turtles, although they stand almost upright like slightly bent-over humans. Usually they are shown with a shell on their back. Their most distinctive characteristic, however, is a cuplike indentation in the top of the head. This must be kept filled with water or the kappa is powerless and may even die. So, if you ever meet a kappa, bow to him. Because he is well mannered, he will return the bow. The water will spill out and you will be safe.

Well, as we said, the kappa at the temple are friendly ones, and people often come to ask their help. The procedure is to buy a small figure of a kappa at the temple office and leave it at the altar. You will recognize the proper place because of the number of kappa figures already there, and the kappa pictured on the money box. Because of course you should drop in a coin or two so that the kappa can hear you clearly. Kappa-dera is reported to be very efficacious in helping supplicants with their business problems. And for those who have difficulty accomplishing their goals, the kappa will provide the extra push that they apparently need.

Now retrace your steps. At the signal, you may notice a long line of trucks lined up, interspersed by men with handcarts. All have the same load—waste paper. You have heard the men who come through your neighborhood in loudspeaker trucks soliciting old paper and magazines in exchange for toilet tissue. Here is where they sell what they collect.

Cross the Kappabashi intersection. On the left, you will see two knife stores, Tokyo Riki Oroshi Center (東京利器卸センター) and Tsubaya Hochoten (つばや庖丁店). Here is a world of specialization, knives of all shapes and sizes, and for every imaginable use. If you are going to slice smoked salmon, your knife must be sharp, and there should be grooves along the blade to catch and hold the oil that is released with the cutting. There are special knives for tomatoes and for asparagus, as well as imported blades, including some American frontier models with bone handles from the Old West.

Shortly beyond, on the left, you will see Fujiya (ふじや製麺所), an old-style udon store which still makes these popular thick noodles at the back of the shop. Are they different from the ones you buy at the supermarket in plastic packages? Probably. Anyone will tell you that they have "Asakusa no aji," the taste of Asakusa. Buy a portion and notice the efficient method used to put the noodles in the plastic bag.

Shitamachi is proud of its craftsmen. There are not many of them anymore, and there will be fewer in the future. Apprentices who are willing to undergo the long and rigorous training period are hard to find. There is concern that in another generation or two these crafts will be only memories.

To record their history, a small museum and library has been established by the Asakusa Tourist Promotion Association.[2] The Tokyo Electric building in which they are located houses a service center for Asakusa residents on the first floor. The second is given over to a display of the works of some of the local craftsmen and the things they make. There are photos, for example, of a maker of portable shrines (mikoshi) at work. Look at them carefully. Soon you will be seeing these elaborate creations in a local shop and will appreciate the demands of his profession.

You may be surprised at the photos that show the making of *katsura,* or wigs, the kinds worn by actors in Edo-period dramas and in Kabuki. The surprise? That the heart of the wig is a metal form made from careful measurements of the wearer's head. It is claimed that the metal base is essential to give it the necessary stability. Watching the strenuous activities of the on-stage actors, you will see why this is a requirement.

You will also see how tabi are made; marvel at the deft fingers of the man who embroiders, with gold thread and silk floss, family crests onto fine silk; and see the processes of inlaying metal and of

2. Asakusa Kogei-kan, 2–27–7 Nishi Asakusa, Taito-ku; tel. 845–3591
   浅草巧芸館　台東区西浅草 2-27-7

making lacquer. (In the old days, boats put out to sea carrying freshly lacquered pieces to dry them in the clean air because of the dust that was constantly being raised in the streets of Edo. One wonders how they cope today.)

The museum is modest, with photos and small displays and exhibits of memorabilia of other Asakusa days. Among them are old movie programs (Shirley Temple in *Little Miss Broadway,* and early Tarzan films) and old prints and pictures, a few of which have been reproduced and are available for sale. There is a library of books, all in Japanese, that recount the history of the area.

The busiest times, you will be told, are when teachers assign homework that demands study of Asakusa history.

Would you like to plan your own festival? Or take home a Shinto shrine? Or perhaps you would like to put a money box, like the kind you see in front of temples, alongside your phone. If so, stop at Miyamoto Taiko.[3] *Taiko* means drums, and that is the main business of this enterprise. Here you can find everything from small hand drums to gigantic festival models, and if what you want is not on display, you can have it made to order.

Visiting this store can be an education. You will see traditional musical instruments such as the *sho,* a sort of miniature hand-held pipe organ used in Bugaku (court music). The small Shinto shrines are like those found in millions of Japanese homes, where family continuity is assured through repetition of ages-old ceremonies, though these days they are often performed in front of the shrine more as a habit than a ritual.

Here is your chance to examine in detail the workmanship involved in making a mikoshi, or portable shrine, such as those you see being jostled about in the streets during festivals when the gods who dwell within are being given an outing through the streets of the neighborhood. It is no wonder that they bear such huge price

3. Miyamoto Taiko, 2–1–1 Nishi Asakusa, Taito-ku; tel. 844–2141
宮本卯之助商店　台東区西浅草 2-1-1

tags, for they represent the highest level of the nation's arts and crafts including lacquer work, weaving, woodworking, and smithery.

There are other things to discover at Miyamoto, such as the wooden blocks that are struck together to accentuate dramatic moments on the Kabuki stage. (Similar ones were used by neighborhood patrols who walked through the streets in the late evening to remind people to put out their charcoal fires before they went to sleep.) There are the special clothes that are worn at festival time, too, and even the red-and-white ropes that are used to mark off special areas. You will find appealing miniatures and Noh masks, carved wooden ones as well as miniature Noh-mask designs embroidered on neckties. Miyamoto too could be considered a museum of Japanese crafts.

We have almost reached the end of our Kappabashi tour, but we would like to suggest one more stop. There are many shops in Tokyo selling antiques and junk. Often we pass on by, hardly glancing toward the crowded, dim interior, or we think, "Next time ..."

Mitoya[4] deserves better, especially if your interest is timepieces. We can't say "clocks," for often other methods of telling time are on display, such as an ancient version in which a trail of burning incense marks the passing of the hours. Old wall clocks tick in pleasing harmony, and a tremendous variety of antique lanterns and light fixtures hang from the ceiling. If you are looking for a gift for a clock lover, don't miss the tie clasps made from the inner workings of a wristwatch.

And now you are almost back where you started, at the Tawaramachi subway station. With a transfer or two, you will soon be back home. Or you can continue your exploration of Shitamachi, where, as we have said so often, you can turn any corner and find yourself in the past.

4. Mitoya, 1–8–14 Nishi Asakusa, Taito-ku; tel. 845–0318
三戸舎　台東区西浅草 1-8-14

Mukojima: Yonder Island

THIS IS THE ISLAND where people went on outings, their excursion into the countryside, when Edo was young. In cherry-blossom time, it was *the place* to stroll along the banks of the Sumida River, or there were lantern-lit boats for hire so that the fragile blossoms could be viewed from the water.

And people still come today, though now they must look over a cement embankment to see the river, and the cherry trees have been planted recently in a city beautification program. Mukojima remains today, as it always has been, one of the traditional places for viewing the blossoms.

It is well worth a visit anytime, even if the cherry trees aren't in bloom, for it retains the feeling of the past.

There are bridges to cross to get to Mukojima. We suggest you start at Kototoibashi (Kototoi Bridge, 言問橋). Cross the bridge and on your right you will see Ushijima Jinja (牛島神社), a shrine that claims a "sacred cow." Actually, it is a bull, and he is made of stone. In fact there are several stone bulls in the compound, but the one you want is in the courtyard. Usually he wears a red bib. And he can bring you many things. If you are suffering from pain or an illness, touch the ailing part and then touch the bull at the same place and he will take on your problem. He is especially competent when it is mental agility that is desired, and he is also supposed to help with business, but I don't know what part you touch to achieve that result. Simply by going there, you assure that you will become a better person. You will notice that many have been there before you for the stone is rubbed smooth.

Once there was a daimyo mansion here, and you can see the garden that the lord so much admired, for this was the country estate of the Mita branch of the Tokugawa family, and they were known for their expertise in the art of garden construction. What was once private grounds are now a public park, open for all to enjoy.

And now a shrine, Mimeguri Jinja (三囲神社). The name means "three times around," and you could hardly be expected to believe the story.

Many years ago, during one of the city's ceaseless construction projects (the city was Edo, not Tokyo, though the perpetual tearing down and rebuilding continues), workmen dug up a jar. When they opened it, they found a small statue inside. And at that moment, a white fox appeared miraculously from nowhere, ran three times around the shrine, and disappeared.

That would be considered a lucky occurrence, and perhaps enough for one small shrine, but there is more.

To the left of the shrine office, behind some bright red torii, you

1. Ushijima Jinja
2. Mimeguri Jinja
3. Kofuku-ji
4. Chomei-ji
5. Yamamoto
6. Kototoi Dango
7. Asahi Beer Hall

will see the stone figures of a man and woman. They were care-
takers at the shrine, and the woman developed magical powers.
She could call up the fox, who would repeat his rounds, bringing
good luck (or granting wishes) to the person who requested his
services. It was only necessary to make a small contribution at the
shrine office. . . . When the woman died, she was permanently
installed in the garden by way of a stone statue, along with her
husband, so that her ability could continue even until today.

And there is still more. This shrine can bring rain. Once, in a period of drought, the farmers were beating on drums in a ceremony beseeching the gods to send them rain. Still the sun beat down mercilessly on the dying rice crops. Then a haiku poet, Kikaku, arrived on the scene. He was so moved by the peasants and their simple faith that he wrote a poem. And *then* it rained. You can see a large stone on which the poem has been carved, and it is said that if you repeat the poem, it will rain. If you want a sunny day for your picnic, don't come here. There is nothing you can do backwards to assure that the sun will shine.

Here too you can make a small pilgrimage. You will notice numbers (in Japanese) on some of the torii, or sacred Shinto gateways. There are seven of them. Twice a year, at the time of the equinox, old people come and walk through the torii for a special blessing: that they will never become so old and decrepit that they will have to rely on their daughters or daughters-in-law to "change their diapers." That may seem strange to Westerners, but in traditional Japan, where families lived together and there was no such thing as a retirement community or a nursing home (and they are still rare), it was the son's wife who cared for the aging parents. Incontinence was considered the greatest indignity, and they still come today, praying it will not happen to them.

To be even more certain, women can buy a special talisman, a wooden *shamoji* (rice server), the one kitchen tool that traditionally is used three times a day in Japanese homes. By using it every day, it will prevent a woman from becoming bedridden and senile. So strong is the association of the shamoji with women's work that it has become the symbol of wifely duties. In more recent years it has also become the symbol for women's demonstrations. For example, when rice prices are raised again, women will march in front of government offices carrying large replicas of shamoji.

Have you seen the shrine on the roof of the great Mitsukoshi Department Store? This is its parent shrine. Years ago, when the first Mitsui came to Edo to seek his fortune, he heard the rain-making story and was greatly impressed. He chose Mimeguri as his family shrine. Now, three times a year, offerings arrive from Mitsui, and once a year the shrine is host to senior officials of the company who come for a special ceremony.

This shrine is dedicated to Ebisu and Daikoku, the so-called "kitchen gods," who are counted among the seven gods of happiness. Ebisu represents the god of wealth and fortune. He is depicted holding a *tai,* a fish whose name also has the connotation of good luck. Daikoku sits on a bale of rice, a symbol of good fortune.

There is a Mukojima tour you can make to six shrines and temples dedicated to these gods of good fortune. We will visit four of them, and if you would like to complete your pilgrimage, ask for a pamphlet at any of the temple or shrine offices and you will be able to find your way from the map that is printed on the back. Neighborhood people will point you in the right direction if you get confused, for they are familiar with the route.

Our next stop is Kofuku-ji (弘福寺), a Zen temple dedicated to Hotei, another god of good fortune. The bag he carries is filled with that commodity, and no matter how much is given away, it remains full. He is always pictured with a huge stomach, a sign of good fortune in days when only the very wealthy could ever afford enough food to create one.

On the right, you will see two figures enshrined, a man and a woman. There was once a Zen priest who was meditating in a remote mountain retreat. But he worried about his parents and missed them very much. To appease his longing, he carved, from stone, figures that represented his mother and father. The local daimyo was very impressed when he heard the story, and later had the figures transferred to his palace, where they were greatly revered. Now they have found a permanent home in this temple.

The mother figure, even though only a carved boulder, looked after her son, and even today it has a reputation for curing coughs and sore throats. It is effective to pay your respects in front of the figures, but for a sure cure you must come during the first week of the New Year when a special cough medicine, made from an old Chinese medicine formula, is sold.

The temple, with its great, soaring roofs, would seem to have been there forever, but actually it is a fairly recent addition. It was rebuilt after the Great Kanto Earthquake of 1923. It survived World War II with only minor damage.

The front is impressive, but don't miss the back. Look for the covered walkway to the left of the main temple building, there to protect the priest in inclement weather when he walks from his quarters to the temple for ceremonies. Look beyond the bridge for a perfect Japanese-style garden.

There is one woman among the happiness gods, Benten, and our next stop, Chomei-ji (長命寺), is dedicated to her. She is the goddess of beauty and music and is greatly revered by geisha, who long for both attributes, but she has a jealous nature. Therefore couples will rarely visit a Benten shrine together, lest her jealousy be aroused, which could bring an end to even the happiest relationship. The snakes that are often seen coiled around her feet represent jealousy. In the old days, it is said, court musicians rarely married. They feared that the goddess Benten would take away their talents if they did.

There is a large stone plaque to the left of the temple. The words are those of the famous poet Basho, writing of the beauty of snow on Mukojima. Basho was a busy poet, composing his poems wherever he traveled, to be rewarded with a night's lodging and his meals. It is a rare place in Japan that does not claim a spot where Basho wrote a poem.

You will be more likely to notice the stone marker with a stone dog curled around its base. He belonged to a sakè dealer, and he is honored here because of his great prowess as a rat catcher. Rats were a troublesome problem in Edo, so his fame lives after him. (And if you have wondered why most trash cans in Japan are blue, it is reported that this is a color that rats dislike intensely.)

The man carved in profile next to this famous dog is Ryuhoku Narihira, a Meiji newspaper editor.

Now, follow the street that goes to the left. It will take you to the banks of the Sumida River. But the banks are cement walls now, and highways sweep overhead. Soon a new bridge will be completed, and there is an entrance to the expressway that heads north to Tohoku. It takes an active imagination to re-create the woodblock-print scenes of people strolling under the cherry blossoms. As we have written, the area is being restored, cherry trees are planted along the shore, and once again people are coming to the riverside for their outings. And when they come, most will stop at Yamamoto[1] for their famous sweet, Chomei-ji *sakura-mochi*. *Sakura* is cherry, *mochi* is rice cake, and Chomei-ji is the nearby temple. People have been buying them for more than 250 years. The cakes must be ordered in advance during the cherry-blossom season, and by the time the first blossom appears, they will be completely sold out for the next week.

The first Yamamoto was a gateman at the temple. After the cherries bloomed, he gathered great quantities of the leaves and pickled them in barrels with salt. Then he wrapped bits of mochi in them. That is the basic recipe that has been followed ever since. It is said he filled thirty-one barrels, and that each barrel contained 25,000 leaves. One wonders who was counting, and whether that many people made excursions to the riverbank and bought his confection.

But you have a choice on Mukojima when it comes to sweets. Of course there is a story. There was a gardener, named Toyama Sakichi, who took advantage of the tempestuous days preceding the Meiji Restoration to buy cheaply the goods of those fleeing from the war-torn capital. He planned to sell them for a profit when things settled down, but they didn't—when the shaky peace was restored, many who had been forced by the shogunate to stay

1. Yamamoto, 5–1–14 Mukojima, Sumida-ku; tel. 622–3262
   やまもと　墨田区向島 5–1–14

in the capital returned to their homes in the country, and there were even larger amounts of things for sale. Pressed for money, Sakichi remembered the story of Yamamoto and his sakura mochi and decided to follow the same path. He adapted a story—it may even have been true—about Narihira, a handsome and wealthy Kyoto nobleman, recounting how he stood beside the Sumida River thinking of his love and wondering if she were thinking of him too. He composed a poem that asked the question. *Kototoi* means to ask a question about something, so Toyama-san's confection was christened *kototoi dango,*[2] and he set up shop near where Narihira had stood, which just happened to be only a few meters down the road from Yamamoto-san's establishment. At least during cherry-blossom time, there is plenty of business for both. If you choose Toyama-san's confection, be sure to notice the framed collection of wooden picks on the wall. When you eat Japanese sweets, a pick is the proper tool to use. As you will see, some of them are well worth collecting.

Now you can stroll along the riverbank. No need to worry about kappa, the little creatures that once pulled unwary children into the river. They could never climb the cement wall that now substitutes for a riverbank.

You can continue your walk to Azumabashi (吾妻橋), where you will see a large Asahi Beer brewery.[3] You can stop at the beer hall next door for "black beer," or draft beer, which is always available.

And if you cross that bridge, you will be close to the boat landing where you can catch the water taxi to Takeshiba Pier near Hamamatsu Station, or you can take either the Ginza or the Asakusa Subway Line.

Or, you could explore another part of Shitamachi, for it surrounds you, in every direction. Just turn at the next corner....

2. Kototoi Dango, 5–5–22 Mukojima, Sumida-ku; tel. 622–0081
   言問団子　墨田区向島 5-5-22
3. Asahi Beer Hall, 1–23–1 Azumabashi, Sumida-ku; tel. 622–0530
   吾妻橋アサヒビヤホール　墨田区吾妻橋 1-23-1

佃
島

Tsukudajima: Paddy Island

THE FORGOTTEN CORNERS of Tokyo—those where "progress" is resisted—become fewer in number, smaller in size. Consequently, our chapter on Tsukudajima will be short. Still, it is important to know that such a place exists, and that the residents there continue to cherish it. Some ninety percent of them have established a solid front to prevent the sale of land which would result in the industrial/apartment-complex sprawl that covers the rest of this largely man-made island in Tokyo Bay.

Island? you might ask. Well, not exactly. Most of you will at one time or another have visited Harumi for some national or international exhibition. On the way there, you crossed two bridges, links between "islands" that were for the most part created in landfill projects. Tsukudajima lies about a kilometer to the left of the first bridge. Though the street is wide, it carries a tremendous burden of truck traffic, and the haze of pollution tends to mask the scenery. One is glad to be past it all, to reach one's destination elsewhere.

Long before landfill enlarged it, Tsukudajima, a natural island in the bay, was an Edo landmark. Then it was used as a training area for undesirables. Here ex-convicts, the few who were eventually released from servitude, were given instruction in trades. Others with even less hope—the outcasts, the poor, the homeless—came here, seeking a way to better their lives.

Toward the end of the Edo period, a new shipyard was built on Tsukudajima. The name may be a familiar one. It was the start of Ishikawajima-Harima Heavy Industries, IHI, the company that devised the technique of building tankers in halves, a method that speeded construction and was the forerunner of the success that Japan was later to enjoy in all major industries. The name Ishikawa is an old one. Ishikawa Hachiemon was given the island during the Kan'ei era (1624–43). At that time, he was a dominant figure in Japan's shipping. One can only wonder if perhaps he had contact with another man whose fame was based on his knowledge of ships —Will Adams, who is better known today for the fictional treatment of his life as Blackthorne in the novel *Shogun*.

Tsukudajima is one of the few places in Tokyo that was not touched by the great earthquake of 1923. There is a legend to explain this miracle. We are told that the local shrine has magic carvings, a dragon and a tiger, that are able to counter disasters. Once in the Meiji era when fire threatened the island, the dragon called for water to fall from heaven while the tiger spit sand at the flames. The fire was quelled. When the fires triggered by the great earthquake raced over Tokyo, residents turned the heads of the dragon and the tiger to face the threatening holocaust, and the

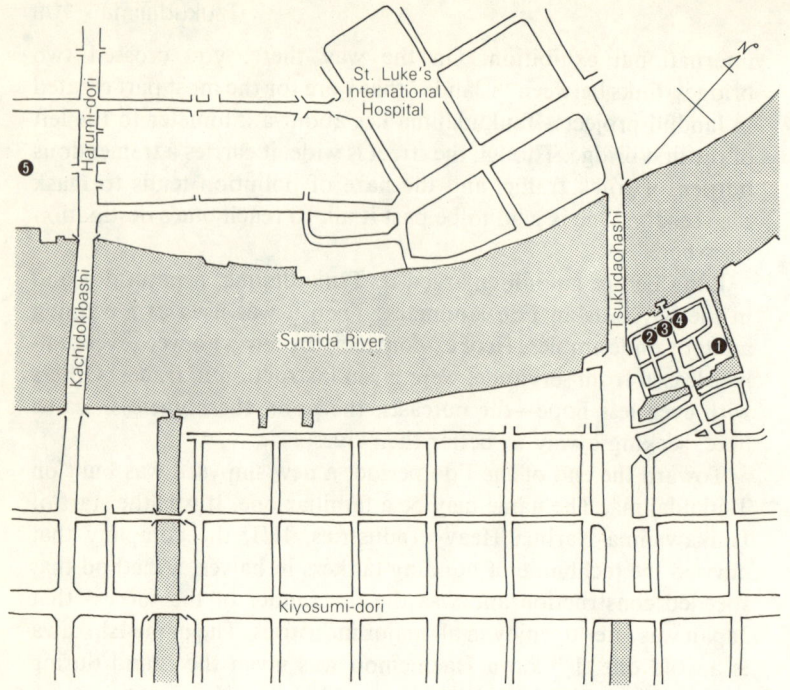

1. Sumiyoshi Shrine
2. Tenyasu
3. Tsukugen
4. Marukyu
5. Tokyo Chuo Oroshiuri Ichiba

flames bowed to a superior power; they turned away from the island.

World War II bombings too spared Tsukudajima, so the island would indeed seem to have some special protection. It celebrates its distinction in a spectacular way, a festival held every three years. Then the black-lacquered, octagonal portable shrine—there isn't another like it in all of Kanto—is carried through the streets and a gigantic flag is hoisted on a pole twenty-five meters high that is usually kept submerged in one of the waterways that lace the island. The flag is called "five-*tan* flag" referring to its width in relationship to a *tan* of fabric used for making kimono, or about 1.75 meters; in length it measured almost twenty meters. No other shrine in Edo was permitted to have such a large flag. You can see how it looked then in Hiroshige's woodblock print of Tsukudajima, in his "One Hundred Views of Edo." There is dancing too, and the Tsukudajima *bon* dance has been awarded the honor of being cited as an intangible cultural asset.

With such a rich history, what is there to see on Tsukudajima today? Not much. Let's cross the Kachidoki Bridge (勝どき橋) near Tsukiji Station on the Hibiya Line. Look over your shoulder, there on your right, and you will see Tokyo's vast fish market (築地魚市場),[1] the subject of the next chapter, an excursion for another day when you can join the shoppers seeking out the freshest produce at what must surely be one of the world's most fascinating wholesale markets.

But now, our destination is Tsukudajima. The Kachidoki Bridge approach is recommended because it allows a gradual introduction to this old neighborhood, and by the time you reach the few remaining streets that still wear the history of Edo, you will have absorbed some of the feeling of this holdout from the past. Perhaps we should warn you. It is a rather long walk....

Take note of the bridge you are crossing. The name means *banzai*. It was completed in 1940, a ten-year project which cost the tremendous sum (then) of four million yen. The center section is a drawbridge, each half weighing about two thousand tons. Five times a day this "tower" was raised—it took only one minute and ten seconds—to allow the passage of vessels in the channel. This accounted for its popular name in those days, the Tower Bridge of Tokyo.

---

1. Tokyo Chuo Oroshiuri Ichiba, 5–2–1 Tsukiji, Chuo-ku; 542–1111
   東京中央卸売市場　中央区築地 5-2-1

But that was yesterday. For many years the traffic on the bridge has far exceeded the passage of ships beneath it, and the flow of motor traffic is far more important to the city's transportation network. Now, too, eleven bridges cross the river between here and Asakusa, and none of the others can be raised. Consequently, river traffic is limited to barges and water buses, and the bridge is never raised.

Cross the bridge and take the first street to the left. Gradually it expands into a shopping street, typical of the neighborhoods of Tokyo, shops selling a wide variety of merchandise. This can be the latest in electronic marvels or the traditional products that were also featured in Meiji times—workmen's clothing, preserved foods, sakè, soy sauce, and miso. There are old shops that now undertake new business too. At one, you can watch T-shirts being made. The cutting is done by hand; they are stitched and finished as you watch; and you can select your own from a table in front of the shop. A handmade T-shirt is rare in these days of mass production.

There is also a supermarket, packaging everything in plastic and featuring come-on specials that threaten the existence of tiny independent shops. Perhaps you will see a street-cart loaded with fish (both preserved and fresh) or household goods or vegetables, their prices a threat even to the supermarket. Red awnings proclaim a bargain sale, foods simmer on grills, there are soba stands, a tiny shrine down a narrow lane, children, balloons, cotton candy—the street wears a festival air on any busy day. But times are changing, and, unlike the past, Sunday is no longer the most crowded. Tsukudajima merchants too like holidays, and only about half of the stores are now open on Sundays. Plan your excursion accordingly. Saturdays would promise the most colorful scene.

And perhaps— do you hear those drums? No, it's not a Buddhist temple rite. Listen carefully and you may recognize the tune. Yes! It's "Onward Christian Soldiers," and around the corner they come, the Salvation Army Band. There is a branch office near by, and Tsukudajima streets have always been hospitable to these crusaders. There are lots of surprises along this shopping street, still firmly anchored in the past.

After you have crossed the highway (or you can start your tour here at Tsukuda Bridge—佃大橋), you will reach the Tsukudajima that you have come to see, the part that remains from the past, hanging in there in spite of the "progress" that is trying to overwhelm it. A favorite destination for painters and pilgrims, these few blocks retain reminders of other, simpler days.

Follow the main street along the waterfront and note three stores, Tsukugen Tanakaya,[2] Tenyasu,[3] and Marukyu;[4] they all sell the island's traditional product, *tsukudani,* seafoods simmered for hours in a soy-sauce mixture until it has been completely absorbed. This was the method used to preserve food in earlier days when the island's fishermen put to sea for days or weeks. Tsukudani assured survival until they returned to port. The shops generally provide samples, but foreigners are not very promising customers. The almost-black fish and sea-vegetables rarely please the Western palate at first taste.

There are old houses weathered by winds and the sea air. And new ones too, balconies set on stucco walls and ornate doors, but old or new, residents are proud of home ownership, and they want to keep their corner of the island exclusively their own.

If it is a nice day, some of the residents will be sharing your pastime, walking along the streets and remembering. They are willing to share their knowledge with the curious. A smile can often be rewarded with a pleasant interlude of remembrances.

Note the copper torii at the edge of the water that proclaims the nearby location of the island's shrine. Cages along the sea

2. Tsukugen Tanakaya, 1–3–13, Tsukuda, Chuo-ku; 531–2649
  佃源田中屋　中央区佃 1-3-13
3. Tenyasu, 1–3–14 Tsukuda, Chuo-ku; 531–3457
  天安　中央区佃 1-3-14
4. Marukyu, 1–2–10 Tsukuda, Chuo-ku; 531–4823
  丸久　中央区佃 1-2-10

wall once held fighting cocks; today's occupants are more docile.

Follow the road leading toward the shrine. You will pass the house of Kinosuke Kaneko, the head of the neighborhood association. Usually, in a box beside his door, you will see brochures (in Japanese) telling some of the history of the island. He also has a remarkable collection of photographs dating back to many festivals of the past. You might notice a small plaque beside the door. It commemorates his brother's spiritual return from the war. Symbolically, he rests at Yasukuni Shrine, where the war dead are enshrined, finally at peace.

At the corner beyond Kaneko-san's house is Sumiyoshi Shrine (住吉神社). Here the carved dragon and tiger continue to protect the heritage of this island. Behind the shrine, submerged in the waters of the canal, is the long pole that holds the five-*tan* flag at festival time. Children play in the parks dotted here and there along the streets, and people stop for lunch at one of the local noodle shops while housewives sweep the streets and discuss the cost of vegetables with their friends. Flowers bloom in bright profusion everywhere, in pots, cans, and plastic buckets that rival the blossoms in their brilliant colors. Fishing boats put out to sea and the makers of tsukudani simmer their catch in some secret blend of soy sauce and seasonings. Life goes on as usual on Tsukudajima, a small corner of Tokyo that resists change.

Tsukiji: Reclaimed Land

YOUR SUBWAY STOP, again, is Tsukiji Station on the Hibiya Line. Subways have become a fast and efficient way of traveling in Tokyo, but much is missed. There is no looking out the window. A good book, or trying to read or reason the advertisements, or observing the other passengers are the popular in-car entertainments. And when your people-watching rewards you with a vista of rubber-booted men boarding the car with baskets full of creatures, often still wriggling, from the sea, you can be reasonably certain that you have arrived at Tsukiji, where the city's fish and produce market is located. To see what greater Tokyo is eating—and to buy it wholesale—surface.

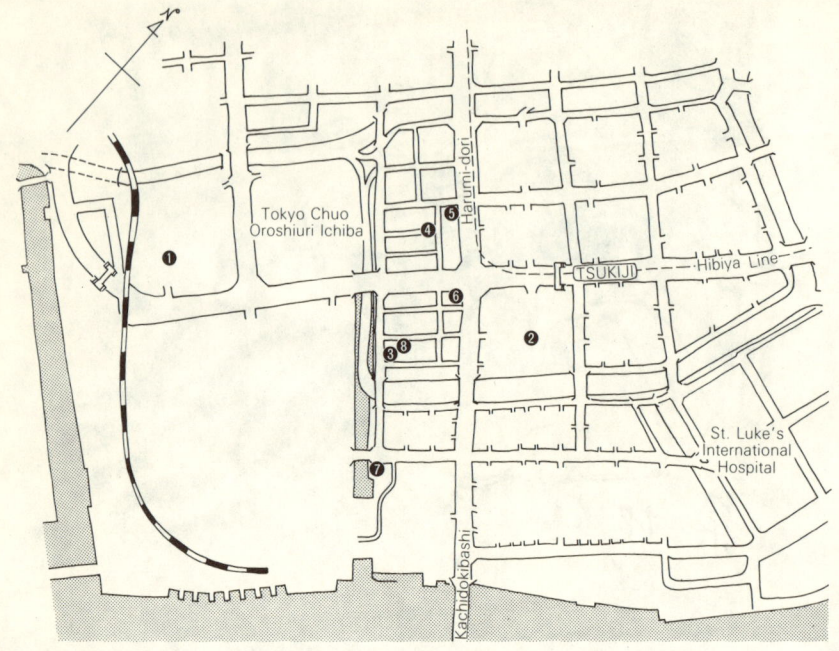

1. Asahi Shimbun
2. Tsukiji Hongan-ji
3. Sushisei
4. Edogin

5. Chikara
6. Segawa
7. Namiyoke Inari Jinja
8. Shoro

Once, where you are standing, there was only water. When Edo was selected as capital for the shogunate, it was necessary to change a village into a city. It was done in record time. The land where Tsukiji is came a little later, after the great fire of 1657 that destroyed so much of the city. The reclamation of land along the harbor became a part of the city planning project. Thus Tsukiji was built. The name literally means "made or reclaimed land."

The waterways extending from the Sumida River became essential for transporting goods. Products from all over Japan arrived at Edo Harbor where they were transferred to *takase-bune,* or barges, to be delivered throughout the city by way of the canals that branched off from the Sumida River. During these early times, the land belonged to Asano Takumi no Kami, the lord of Aki, whose name is commemorated in the story of the forty-seven ronin. (See Shinagawa chapter, *Foot-loose in Tokyo.*)

After the Meiji Restoration, the doors of Japan were opened to foreigners, and many of them came. They were not always welcome, and it was felt to be expedient to keep them as segregated as possible. A foreign settlement was created at Tsukiji, which at the time was little more than mud flats at the mouth of the Sumida River. It was already cut off from the rest of the city by canals, and now a great wall was constructed on the river side, the stones similar to those that formed the walls at the palace. This served to isolate the area even more completely, and both surveillance and protection were simplified. Obviously, it was a perfect choice for a foreign settlement.

Foreigners employed by the Japanese government and diplomatic personnel were allowed to live in the city proper, but for some thirty years Tsukiji was to be home for the others. It is recorded that in 1871 only 12 foreigners were living there but by 1898 the number had grown to 199. In the short span of time during which it existed, a Western-looking city, incongruous with the world around it, was established.

Most of the residents were missionaries, the traders preferring the more hospitable port of Yokohama. Tsukiji was considered to be an unhealthy place to live, and at ebb tide, the lowlands were laid bare "under the noses of the community," as one observer noted at the time. At its zenith, there were four churches, two legations, three seminaries, a hospital, a hotel, a butchery, a half-dozen parsonages, and, rather surprisingly, an orphanage. There were no guards to keep people in or out, and it is reported that many Japanese sought the help of resident missionaries in order to learn English, and were rewarded with a generous amount of scriptural training along with their language instruction. Then, as now, many young people went to church to study English.

For Isabella Bird, whose *Unbeaten Tracks in Japan* records her impressions of the country in 1878, Tsukiji had little appeal: "The roads are broad and neatly kept, but the aspect of the Concession is dull and desolate, and people live near enough to each other to be hourly fretted by the sight of each other's dreary doings."

So much for the Tsukiji foreign settlement. In 1899 a new treaty allowed foreigners to live anywhere in Tokyo, and even before that date some residents had been permitted to live elsewhere. The neat little town was soon abandoned.

But something remains. St. Luke's International Hospital (聖路加病院) traces its roots to one of the early settlement hospitals. Once you could see its tower, topped with a golden cross, from anywhere in the area; now you can spot it from the top of the pedestrian overpass by the subway exit. The building you *can* spot from (almost) anywhere today belongs to the *Asahi Shimbun,* one of Japan's largest newspapers, with a circulation of twelve million.

Our guide to history completed, we will now proceed with our tour. Wherever you exit, you will see the imposing Tsukiji Hongan-ji (築地本願寺), a temple founded in 1630 and destroyed repeatedly by fire, the last time in the 1923 earthquake. The present building, built in Hindu style, is claimed to be disaster proof.

(If you are planning a trip to Kyoto, visit the main Hongan-ji temple, Nishi Hongan-ji, only a short walk from the station. Here is one of the wonders of Japan, a building from the lavishly decorated palace-complex of Hideyoshi. It is said that he accepted three bids for the building and took the highest. "You get what you pay for," he is reported to have explained. And he did get it, as you can see today. Ask at the temple office to join one of the tours through the temple. It will include this magnificent building.)

Now it is time to explore the market you have come to see. Early risers have the best view, for the fish auctions start around 5 A.M. There will still be a lot to see if you come at 7 A.M. or even later, but certainly plan to complete your tour by noon. After that time, many of the shops will begin to close for the day.

The large fish are sold to secret signals that are incomprehensible to nonprofessionals. Be alert when the auction is over and buyers begin to haul out their purchases. This is one of the few times in Japan that the visitor is not an honored guest. He is simply in the way. In recent years, many of the handcarts used to take fish to the waiting trucks have been replaced by motorized haulers, and visitors must be ready to move fast. If you bought a charm at Suitengu in Ningyo-cho, be sure you bring it with you. That's the one that protects you from being splashed by water.

The auction market is alongside the dock. Inside the building, laid out in a vast still-life, is an astonishing array of seafoods, many of which you may hope never to find on your table. It is a marvel of variety and color, many of the creatures still very much alive, because everyone knows seafood must be fresh to be good. At most of these stalls, proprietors will good-humoredly sell to individuals for their own kitchens, and many Tokyo residents come here when they want the freshest produce in the city.

If you can't wait to get home with whatever you buy, search the neighboring streets for a sushi shop—you won't have to look far— and have a breakfast of the freshest fish in town. Here is a brief guide to some of the most popular ones though everyone claims a favorite and you can hardly make a mistake wherever you go.

Closest to the fish market is Sushisei,[1] a small shop claiming a ninety-year history. It seats only about fifteen customers, and the fact that there are usually three times that number standing in line testifies to its popularity.

1. Sushisei, 4–13–9 Tsukiji, Chuo-ku; 541–7720
   すし清　中央区築地 4-13-9

Edogin[2] is a complex of several shops, each with its own characteristics. It has always been popular with foreigners. For one reason, a picture menu with prices makes ordering easy.

Near the station is Chikara.[3] You may be reminded of your favorite New York saloon when you see the counter of dark, polished wood, but no New York establishment could fill a glass counter behind the bar with such a wide variety of seafood.

Finally, at the Tsukiji intersection there is a tiny shop, Segawa,[4] in business for some sixty years, with only four ancient stools and a fold-down shelf for a counter. We suggest that you go first to the fish market before exploring the other streets of Tsukiji because the earlier you go the more you will see, but you may want to stop here on your way because it usually closes well before noon, and you will find only a battered shutter pulled down over the minute workspace. All that is served is *maguro* (tuna), reportedly the best available that day. The clientele is loyal, a constant coming and going where the counter is always full but you never have to wait long for a seat. No one lingers after finishing, for there is far too much business to be done. There is no luxury but plenty of atmosphere, and the price can best be described as cheap.

As you leave the fish market, look for the small shrine just beyond one of the bridges that crosses the canal, a few tall trees pinpointing its location. Namiyoke Inari Jinja (波除稲荷神社) it is called, and the name signifies its mission. It expresses the feeling of calm seas, the kind that fishermen like best, and the shrine can assure them.

There is a legend. The shrine was first built some three hundred years ago. It was a time when there were great difficulties; things weren't going at all well. What the problems were is not clear, but

2. Edogin, 4–5–1 Tsukiji, Chuo-ku; 543–4401
   江戸銀　中央区築地 4-5-1
3. Chikara, 4–4–14 Tsukiji, Chuo-ku; 543–2817
   力　中央区築地 4-4-14 ラフィネ東銀座 207号
4. Segawa, 3–8 Tsukiji, Chuo-ku; 542–8878
   瀬川　中央区築地 3-8

they involved the land. We know it was only mud flats at best in those ancient days and it probably had to do with the big reclamation project after the fire. At any rate, someone saw something shining in the waters. We don't know what it was, but it was installed as a *kamisama*—a god—at this small shrine, and after that there were no more problems with the land. This is now the shrine for all of the Tsukiji area. (It is interesting to note that there is no place in Japan that is not "protected" by some shrine. Tall buildings often have a shrine on the roof to help them keep in touch. They don't want to be too far away from its influence.)

Passers-by, the fishermen, and those who work at the market—and customers too—often pause a few moments to offer a prayer in front of the shrine, a moment of quiet in a busy day. They ask for more than calm seas, however. For continued success it is necessary to express appreciation to the many creatures from the seas that make the market a profitable endeavor. Their spirits also must be considered in the master plan of things, and you too might want to express your appreciation for their sacrifice, for without it, there would be no Tsukiji, no sushi shops, and no fresh fish on tonight's menu.

Between the Tsukiji intersection and the fishmarket are narrow lanes filled with shops selling almost anything a cook or his helper might ever want. Mainly it is produce, fresh fruits and vegetables, with emphasis on pre-season specialties, but there is much more: dried foods such as mushrooms and octopus, an endless variety of nuts and sembei, tea and seaweed, and things you may never see anywhere else again.

Some products are typically Japanese like *tamago-yaki,* a sweet, heavy, custard-like egg concoction that serves as "dessert" at sushi shops. One wonders who the customers are since the quality of the tamago-yaki served is supposed to be a key to the ability of a sushiya-san, and each claims to make his own. Yet many send their apprentices to the tamago-yaki makers of Tsukiji. All have their regular customers. If they don't arrive by the time the shop closes, usually around noon, their order will be left on the counter to be picked up at some convenient time. The shopkeeper, up long before dawn mixing eggs and cooking the thin layers that comprise the blocks, is ready for a nap.

There are many tamago-yaki dealers in the area, but one of the best is Shoro.[5] Before World War II it was a sushi shop but the building was destroyed during the firebombing. They use ten thousand eggs a day to make the thousand blocks of tamago-yaki they sell to their customers. You can buy one of the blocks for less than you pay for the large slice that is sold at most grocery stores.

There are many other things to shop for in Tsukiji. Even today, many knives are made by craftsmen, not factories. They may demand more care—more sharpening and polishing—but if you pause to watch a master chef slice the fish for his tiny works of art, you will know his knives must be the best. They are, and he probably buys them at one of the knife stores in Tsukiji. At the same shop you will probably find scissors, the kind shaped like grass clippers, in all sizes, some so tiny they will fit in your coin purse. If you have Japanese women friends, you have probably been surprised at the number of helpful things they always seem to have on hand: a tiny towel for wiping hands, a plastic bag to put damp things in, and always a tiny pair of scissors for emergencies. Surprise your friends, and be first to produce a pair from your handbag to clip a raveling or the corner of a plastic bag that resists all efforts to open it.

Workman's clothes are featured at some of the shops, as well as cover-all aprons, uniforms for waiters at Japanese-style restaurants, cotton towels with pleasing patterns, and shirts, equally appropriate for men or women, in attractive Japanese designs. At other shops you will find twine, lacquer and plastic trays and serving

5. Shoro, 4–13–13, Tsukiji, Chuo-ku; 543–0582
   松露　中央区築地 4-13-13

pieces, and containers of all kinds. Each street will produce a new display as you walk up one and down another, and let's try that narrow cross street over there.

And as you complete your tour of Tsukiji, you can wonder again at how much things change while still remaining the same. From earliest times, this area has served to supply the city with the produce it requires. The barges no longer make deliveries by way of the canals and instead people come by subway, taxi, and truck to make their purchases. Buildings have been modernized many times, but changes are generally unnoticed because interest is focused far more on the products that are sold than on the shops that sell them. Goods spill out over the narrow walks, and shopkeepers, tenugui twisted and tied around their heads, shout out their welcome as they urge you to stop and look at the best bargains in Tsukiji. Just as they did in countless yesterdays.

Now there is talk of building a modern fish market, perhaps in a different location on new fill land in the southern part of the city, nearer to Tokyo Harbor. So Tokyo goes on, destroying and rebuilding, but always leaving a little of the past for those who would search for it in the back streets of Shitamachi . . . or anywhere.

*   *   *

Like, for example, Narita, the city nearest to the New Tokyo International Airport, most often referred to as Narita Airport to differentiate it from Haneda, which serves domestic lines. This can hardly be called Shitamachi no matter how far we extend the borders, but it is an area rich in history and legend. Since few people can come to Japan without having some story to tell about their own airport experience, we decided to include Narita in this book. Then when you talk about Narita, you can tell about an early hero who sacrificed his life for his village, a prayer wheel that mass produces blessings, and one of the most beautiful parks in this part of Japan. But that is only a beginning. Few people realize how much more there is to see at Narita than the airport. . . .

成田

Narita: Paddies of Abundance

YOU MAY BE VISITING JAPAN, you may be living here, but either way, it is highly unlikely that your fondest thoughts of this nation will in any way be centered on the Tokyo International Airport at Narita. It has never been able to count many friends.

The opening date was delayed (with considerable official embarrassment) when radicals, dedicated to opposing the Japanese establishment with its top priorities going to industrial expansion, evaded the tight security and methodically smashed up the control tower only a few days before the inaugural ceremonies were scheduled.

Idealistic students have joined the few remaining farmers who have refused to relinquish their land to stage continuing demonstrations to oppose the still-incomplete facility that was finally opened in May 1978. Their ranks are sometimes augmented by professional dissidents whose more radical tactics are often unwelcome. Although the farmers want their land back and the students support their goals, they do not want to endanger the lives of those who fly in and out of Narita.

This has resulted in a truce. Demonstrations are expected at certain times, for example, the anniversary of the day the airport opened. At other times, the firm hand of the law is apparent as uniformed riot police stand guard and careful passenger screening is conducted at the entrance gate. Observant passengers will also see certain areas beyond the runways set off by barbed wire. This is land which is surrounded by airport property but has not yet been surrendered by the owner. In the meantime, he is assured entrance to his fields but is cut off from the airport property.

Viewing the scene, some might think they were visiting a nation at war instead of one that stands firpipe committed to peace.

But there is more. Nearby residents fought the construction of a pipeline to carry fuel, and foreign-airline officials complain that the unprecedentedly high cost of construction has made refueling at Narita the most expensive in the world.

In addition, complaints are continually being lodged against the inevitable noise from jet engines, and local entrepreneurs are suffering because the anticipated business boom has yet to develop.

And finally, the cloud of a scandal that has never been deeply probed lies over the decision to locate the airport across the bay from Tokyo in the fertile Chiba farmlands, and the ensuing land purchases.

But the loudest cry comes from those who use the facilities for their intended purpose, to fly into and out of Japan.

"It took me longer to get into Tokyo than it did to fly from Hong Kong," is a common complaint. Or from Korea. Or Taiwan.

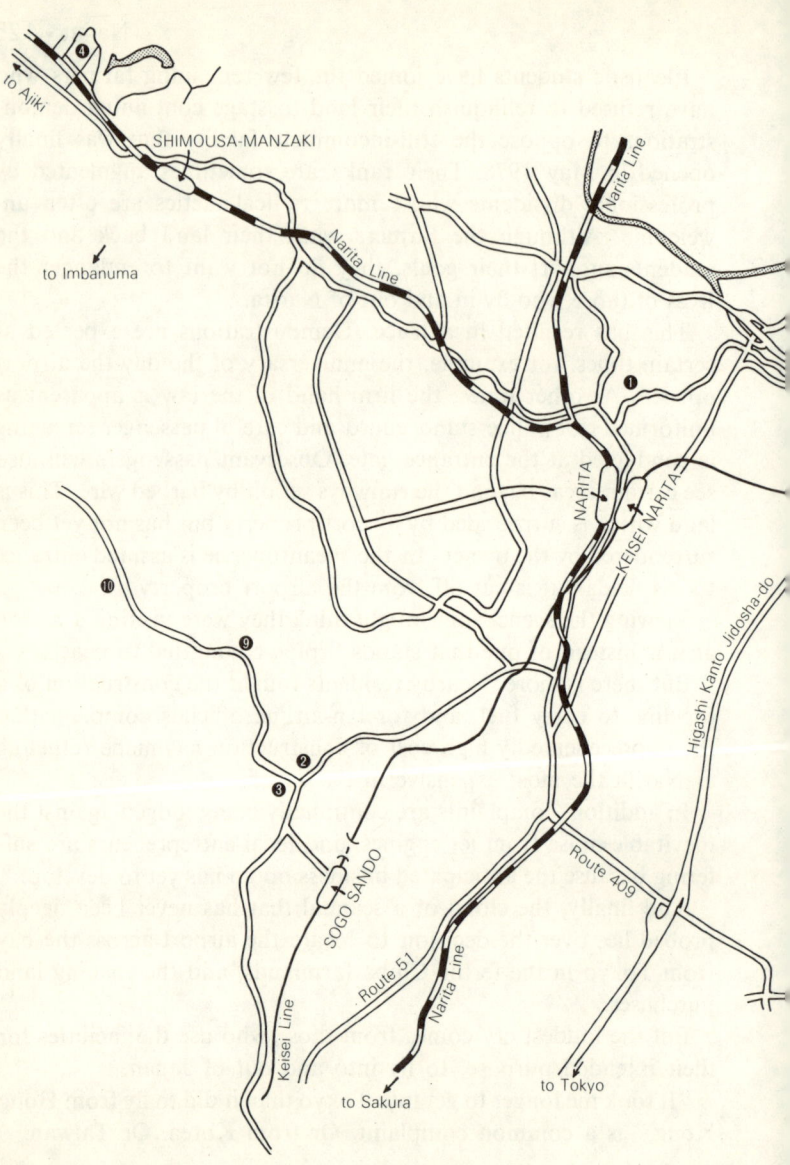

to Ajiki

SHIMOUSA-MANZAKI

to Imbanuma

Narita Line

Narita Line

NARITA

KEISEI NARITA

Higashi Kanto Jidosha-do

SOGO SANDO

Keisei Line

Route 51

Route 409

Narita Line

to Sakura

to Tokyo

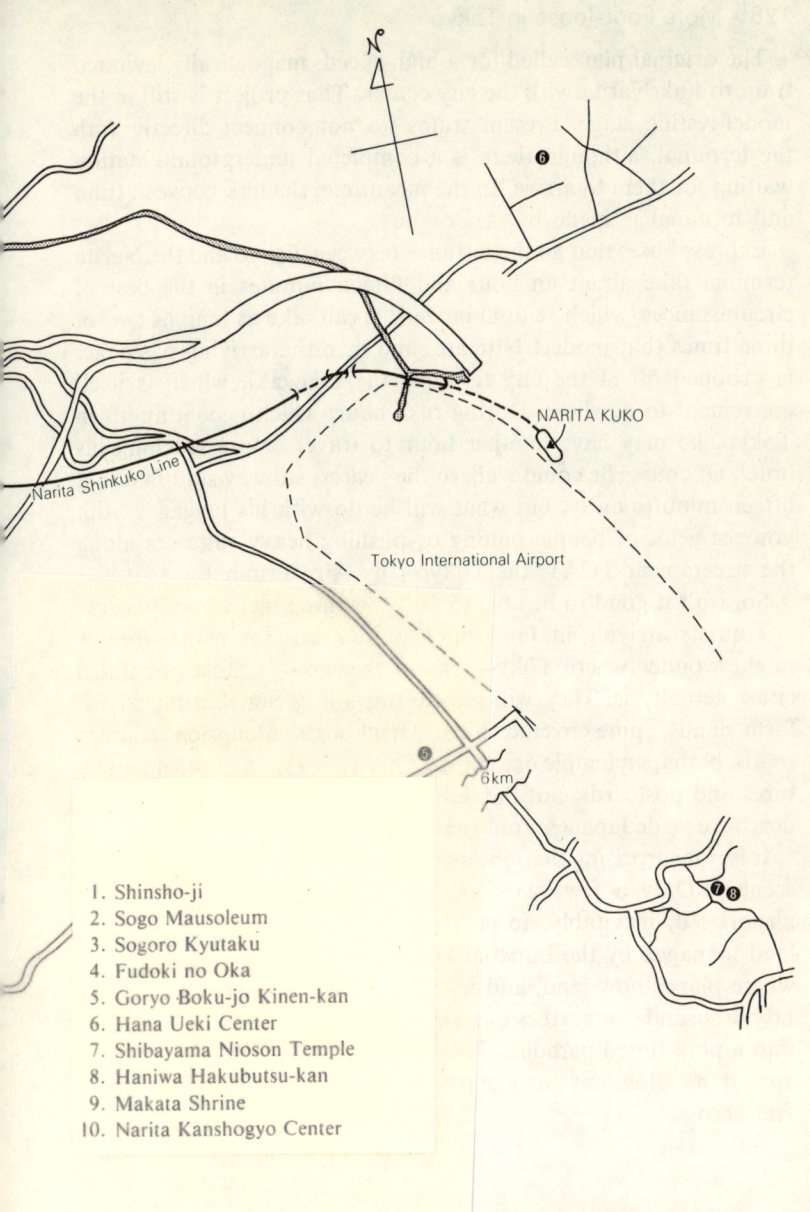

N

❻

NARITA KUKO

Narita Shinkuko Line

Tokyo International Airport

❺

6km

❼❽

1. Shinsho-ji
2. Sogo Mausoleum
3. Sogoro Kyutaku
4. Fudoki no Oka
5. Goryo Boku-jo Kinen-kan
6. Hana Ueki Center
7. Shibayama Nioson Temple
8. Haniwa Hakubutsu-kan
9. Makata Shrine
10. Narita Kanshogyo Center

The original plan called for a high-speed, magnetically levitated train to link Narita with the city center. That project is still in the model-testing stage. Present trains do not connect directly with the terminal, although there is a completed underground station waiting for them to arrive. In the meantime, the link between train and terminal is made by taxi or bus.

Express buses that go the distance between Tokyo and the Narita terminal take about an hour and fifteen minutes in the best of circumstances, which seldom prevail. It can take as long as two or three times that modest estimate, and then the arriving passenger is dropped off at the city terminal in Hakozaki, which is itself convenient to nowhere. During rush hour, which is continuous in Tokyo, he may have another hour to travel before reaching his hotel. Of course he could walk to the nearest subway station about fifteen minutes away, but what will he do with his luggage? Still, you see a lot of people pulling or pushing heavy suitcases along the streets near TCAT, the Tokyo City Air Terminal.

So, isn't it good to be able to say something nice about Narita?

Tourists arriving in Japan and looking out the plane window might wonder where Tokyo, one of the world's most populated cities, actually is. They will see contrasts in green that mark rich farm lands, pine-covered hills, farmhouses alongside country roads, perhaps a temple or a shrine. This is the Japan of calendar pictures and postcards, not the industrial giant whose quality products have made Japanese trade names familiar throughout the world.

It is not surprising that one's first glimpse of Japan projects rural scenery. Only a few years ago, before the negotiations for an airport led, inevitably, to reality, this was the emperor's pasture land managed by the Imperial Household Agency. Horses grazed where planes now land, and in the spring—ah, spring in Japan—fifty thousand cherry trees burst into bloom, turning the farm lands into a pink-tinted paradise. There was one umbrella-type tree that spread its blossoms in a shower of petals that was forty-eight feet across.

For some people, Narita is no more than a stopover on their way to somewhere else. Yet, even without the airport, the area would be a destination worth seeking out, for here you can find the "real Japan" that many have come so far to discover (and often never find). It has wide appeal—for the tourist with a few hours between planes as well as residents of Japan who want something beyond the standard guidebooks. Some may even decide to stay on, spending the night at a friendly *ryokan* (Japanese inn) along the country-village streets so close—and yet so far—from Tokyo's international airport.

There is much more to see than rural scenery. Chiba Prefecture, where Narita is located, is rich in history. In the ancient days, when legend is gradually blending into fact, it is recorded that Jimmu Tenno, Japan's first emperor, sent military forces here from the Yamato court near Nara under his most powerful warrior to subdue the indigenous population, the Caucasian Ainu, or Ezo as they were called then. The campaign was successful, and the local clans were driven away, finally being pushed as far north as Hokkaido, where their descendents still live today.

And from more ancient times, the lakes and swamps around Narita occasionally yield a record of prehistory in the bones of now-extinct animals.

With such a long time span to consider, it is not surprising that there are many sites to see. The orientation point for our travels is the JNR (Japanese National Railways) station in Narita City, reached by train from Tokyo Station in about an hour and a half, or by bus from the airport, about twenty-five minutes. Buses stop at the JNR station. There is another station nearby. Don't confuse them. If you are planning to return to the airport, your bus will leave from in front of the JNR station.

There are taxi and bus stops in front of the station. For most buses, you are expected to take a ticket from the dispenser as you board. Hand it in when you leave, along with the fare. Carry some change; bus drivers don't break bills. Looking receptive (or confused) will inevitably prompt offers of assistance from the Japanese who will help you get where you want to go (just point to the kanji in the book). You might even find an English-speaking companion for your travels.

Narita traces its name to a legend. It is derived from the word *naruta,* which means "rice paddies where thunder is often heard." The noise decreased remarkably after a Buddhist deity, Fudo Myoo, was enshrined in the village temple. As a consequence, the rice harvest increased spectacularly. To commemorate this, the name was changed from Naruta to Narita, or "rice paddies with high yields." The Fudo deity, personified in images of wood or stone, has always been capable of performing miracles.

But old stories are never simply told, and a curious reader might wonder why the Fudo was installed in the temple.

It was a long, long time ago, in the year 940 or thereabouts, that a rebellion broke out in what was then known as Naruta. There was a Fudo statue in a Kyoto temple that was revered for its supernatural powers and the emperor decided to send it—along with troops—to restore peace. The battle was soon won, and plans were made to return the deity to his home in Kyoto.

Then a strange thing happened. The local laborers were unable to move it. Each time they tried, it seemed miraculously to increase in weight till no human could lift it. This was interpreted as meaning that the Fudo liked it there, and he was allowed to stay, a special temple being built for him. Apparently there was no transportation problem when the statue—and the temple—were moved to the present site in 1705.

Narita-san, or Shinsho-ji (新勝寺),[1] the temple where you can almost see the Fudo statue, is only a short downhill walk from the train station along an old, narrow road. With only scant imagination, you can feel that you are traveling back into the past, the

1. Shinsho-ji, 1 Narita, Narita-shi; 0476–22–2111
   新勝寺　成田市成田 1

ancient pilgrims' path leading you into a traditional woodblock print. The slope is lined with open-front shops where hawking salespeople urge you to buy their goods. A hundred years ago, temple visitors were similarly tempted to reach into their purses for the coins that would purchase the specialities of the area.

Watch for an old drugstore, Mitsuhashi,[2] just beyond the temple entrance. Among its aspirin and vitamin drinks, you will find displays of Chinese medicine, and packets of the beauty aid *uguisu no fun* (nightingale droppings) which you read about in the Asakusa chapter. You can replenish your supply if what you bought then has been depleted. The proprietor will welcome you with a few words in English, meticulously written on a note pad. Mitsuhashi-san's hearing has failed, but not his hospitality. Write a big "HELLO!" on the paper to begin your own personal experience with Narita. Notice his wife's beautiful complexion, attributable, perhaps, to nightingale droppings.

"Irasshai!" (welcome), the shopkeepers call out as you walk along the street. Most of the shops feature a curious array of pleasingly packaged foods that are not too familiar to the West—Japanese-style pickles and *yokan* (sweet bean-paste) as well as sakè and sembei rice crackers. There are samples for tasting to assure that customers will be happy with what they take home.

Several Japanese-style inns have been accomodating pilgrims and other travelers for some 350 years. One, the Umeya,[3] will serve a tempura or other typical Japanese lunch in your own private room, an introduction to the Japanese way of entertaining: seated on the tatami-matted floor on a silken cushion at a low table, admiring the garden without and the flower arrangement within, and being served by a helpful waitress who will pour your sakè and beer and praise your skill with chopsticks.

2. Mitsuhashi, 363 Nakano-cho, Narita-shi; 0476–22–0011
   三橋　成田市中野町 363
3. Umeya, 376 Nakano-cho, Narita-shi; 0476–22–0003
   梅屋　成田市中野町 376

She may also tell you that the inn received the town's third telephone.

"You can tell by the number, ending in 0003." she explains. "The first went to the temple, the second to the post office, and the third to our inn, the Umeya."

There are other ryokan on the main street. The Oonoya[4] was later to get a phone (0476–22–0007) but may be first to catch your attention with its impressive bell tower. The Wakamatsu (0476–22–1136),[5] built to look like an Edo-style mansion, is directly across from the temple. All will accommodate foreign guests although the Wakamatsu is probably best prepared to do so.

Narita-san is built on a hill. As you enter the main gate at the bottom, the temple appears to be rising up into the clouds. You can call on Fudo, enshrined in the main hall, but unless your eyes have been trained to see in the dark, he will not be visible. Perhaps you will be able to glimpse a hand that sometimes catches the light. It is holding a rope to tie off any evils. They can be stupidity, ignorance, or bad thoughts. In his other hand, he holds a sword, dedicated to the same mission—cutting away the evils which otherwise might envelop us.

"These days," a priest explains, "we have many anxieties. In making a living, we must often deal with people and situations we find unpleasant. We must say goodbye to those we love, must be cordial to many that we do not. This causes anxiety. We must ask for Buddha's help. Fudo will rid you of these anxieties."

If you are there at the right time, you will see a lot of these evils going up in smoke at a goma ceremony held several times a day within the temple. Perhaps you noticed the tables in front of the temple where people were filling out forms. They were listing their "anxieties." Depending on the seriousness of the problem and the

4. Oonoya, 371 Nakano-cho, Narita-shi; 0476–22–0007
   大野屋　成田市中野町 371
5. Wakamatsu, 355 Hon-cho, Narita-shi; 0476–22–1136
   若松屋　成田市本町 355

size of the wooden plaque purchased at the temple entrance on which your name and problem/wishes will be recorded, your petition will cost a few hundred yen or several thousand. Later a priest will hold your plaque in the smoke from the *goma* fire and you will be freed of your evil desires—or, the modern interpretation, have your wishes granted.

And to be truthful, not so many petitioners come to have their evils destroyed. People have very human desires—they want money, a husband, a wife, a baby, a happy home, to pass a university examination. . . . These are the most common requests and because the priests know how busy people are these days, they have a number of pre-blessed plaques—they have already been passed through the holy smoke—that can be effective immediately, the appropriate request already inscribed. There is no need to wait for the next ceremony. Just pay your money to have your name written on the plaque that spells out your need. There is even one that covers everything. Just write your name and pay your money. Then all your dreams will come true.

In fact, a lot of money is paid to the temple, which accounts for many of the elaborate new buildings, including a Chinese-style structure at the top of the hill, built to house the temple's treasures. The temple is also known for its automobile blessings—buy a charm to see you and your car safely through the coming year. Japanese flock to temples on New Year's Eve to assure the dispelling of any evils inclined to hang on from the past, and Narita-san is among the most popular, counting more than three million worshipers during the first days of January. Many come to buy the automobile safety charm. At three thousand yen it is far cheaper than insurance, and it is comforting to know that it is always there, perhaps dangling from the rear-view mirror, protecting you from accidents. They are on sale at the office to the right of the main worship hall where the Fudo is enshrined. And if you are in a hurry (the temple is well aware of the times), you can buy a cheaper version from a vending machine.

There is even a hurry-up blessing arrangement, yours for a contribution of only one hundred yen. A huge, revolving prayer-wheel holds thousands of sutras. Rotating it three times is equivalent to reading all of them. The old priest who tends the wheel—and reminds you to put your one hundred yen coin in the box—will tell you that the Dalai Lama sent the sutras to Japan in 1731. Many of them were produced on woodblocks that are now lost or hidden away in some remote Tibetan monastery. He sums up his story: "They are a treasure."

Or you can show your devotion through *ohyakudo mairi,* a hundred trips around the main temple. It will earn you a special blessing. You will see other pilgrims making their rounds, keeping count by bending down a stiff twist of paper as they complete each circle. Go with a friend, and fifty times around will be enough.

If there are other petitions, they can be saved for Setsubun, the first day of spring (by the old calendar) in February when bean-throwing symbolizes the casting out of evil. In homes throughout Japan, people scatter beans inside their houses as they shout, "Fuku wa uchi, oni wa soto" (in with the good luck, out with the demons). Many temples host bean-throwing ceremonies, usually with some popular entertainer—a sumo star, a singer—tossing the beans to the crowds gathered below. Catching a bean or two assures good luck. Narita-san omits the last part of the chant, the words that order the demons to leave. "There are no demons on temple grounds," the priests explain.

On almost any day, stalls are set up at the temple entrance selling food, souvenirs, and chances—try to catch a goldfish in a paper sieve, fire a cork gun at that bottle of Scotch, buy a box, wrapped and tied, hoping that it holds something more precious than your good sense tells you it will.

Turn toward the left from the main hall and you can continue to explore the vast grounds. If you go up the slope to the right, you will enter a different world, the Naritasan Natural Park (成田山公園), an expanse of forty-five acres that celebrates each season in its scenery. Paths wind through the woods and alongside the ponds, each turn revealing another postcard-pretty view. Such large and generally uncrowded pathways are rare in Japan. Relax, and enjoy the scenery.

Adjacent to the park is the Naritasan Historical Museum,[6] with folkcrafts and mementos of olden days. Many, including a series of picture panels, relate to the life of the local hero, Kiuchi Sogoro, a village headman who sacrificed his life for his people.

Some three-hundred years ago, the farmers were greatly oppressed by the harsh treatment and heavy taxes imposed by the ruling Sakura clan. Sogoro disobeyed the law and took their petition for relief directly to the shogun, knowing his cause was just while also being well aware of the consequences of his act. The shogun recognized both principles. The farmers were given relief from the oppressive taxes and regulations, and Sogoro and his family were executed. Sogoro was crucified and his four children were decapitated.

You can visit (by foot, taxi, or bus) the Sogo Mausoleum (宗吾霊堂) where his sacrifice is shown in life-sized reproductions, starting with a scene at the castle depicting the wanton life of Lord Sakura, and finally the execution ground, surrounded by weeping villagers. Nearby is the Sogo Biography Hall, which preserves mementos of Sogoro's life as well as historical items contributed by people living in the area, among them a splendid Navy uniform and a jinrikisha.

If you didn't have time at Narita-san, or if you feel you did not rid yourself of all evils, you can arrange for a goma ceremony at this temple too.

On the way out, pause at the stand at the left of the entranceway and sample some of the delicacies of the area, such as eel bones

6. Naritasan Reiko-kan, Narita Koen-nai, Narita-shi; 0476–22–0234
成田山霊光館　成田市成田公園内

salted and deep-fried, or grasshoppers preserved by long, slow cooking in soy sauce, sakè, and sugar. If you look a bit squeamish, the proprietor will assure you that there is no cause for dismay.

"All our grasshoppers come from the rice paddies," she will explain. Their diet, one supposes, is therefore controlled.

Nearby is another sight worth seeing, though one local guidebook only allows two minutes at Makata Shrine (麻賀多神社) to admire what is claimed to be the biggest Japanese cedar (*sugi*) in all of the Kanto district. It is more than twelve hundred years old, and before it was damaged by lightning, it reached twenty-seven meters into the sky.

Our next stop is the site of Sogoro's house.[7] The present building was reconstructed in 1820. Descendants of the family still live there today, but you are welcome to go inside the spacious, dirt-floored front room. Notice the great smoke-darkened beams that span the roof, the raised platform for the tatami-matted rooms within. There is a family altar on a shelf where offerings are still made to the famous hero, and many old folkcrafted artifacts. There are also a television set, a washing machine, and a refrigerator, but progress does permit conveniences that Sogoro-san could never even have dreamed of. Today his villagers are doing very well indeed.

Now a diversion, Narita Fish Land, or Narita Kanshogyo Center.[8] Very few of the fish that are raised here (carp and goldfish) are for eating, however. The finest go to collectors, who gladly pay a million yen or more for a carp that will be the envy of other connoisseurs. They will live pampered lives in some of Japan's most exclusive garden pools. The center is noted for its "brocade" varieties, and the breeders are so skillful that they accept advance orders for special combinations of colors.

7. Sogoro Kyutaku, 569 Daikata, Narita-shi; 0476–26–2097
    惣五郎旧宅　成田市台方 569
8. Narita Kanshogyo Center, 1379 Daikata, Narita-shi; 0476–26–9111
    成田観賞魚センター　成田市台方 1379

Carp have a good image in Japan. Because they can swim upstream, defying strong currents and even waterfalls—as you will see in many traditional Japanese paintings—they have come to signify courage and stamina. That is why on Boys' Day in May you will see huge carp banners (*koi nobori*) "swimming" in the wind above houses and even business institutions, where they perhaps serve to instill male workers with old-time virtues.

Not all the carp are expensive. If it has been a good year, and the hatch is large, baby carp can be bought for as little as five to twenty yen each, if you buy in lots of a thousand. There is always the chance that one of the nondescript babies will be a breeder's delight as a rare combination of colors or characteristics.

Goldfish, too, are available in many varieties. If you don't want to select your fish from those on display, you can try your luck and fish for them, though your catch will be limited to two kilograms. (If you wonder what fifty kilograms of fish would look like, ask to see the giant carp that supposedly weighs that much.)

And for even more excitement, don't miss the pond out beyond the kiddy cars where you can buy a cupful of food and feed the fish. Instantly the surface of the water will be broken with flashes of color as the fish congregate for the feast.

The center also stocks all kinds of fish-keeping supplies, from simple bowls for a child's first goldfish to temperature-controlled aquariums for professionals. The staff can also answer all of your questions about fish raising as long as the conversation is in Japanese.

Now you can return to Narita City, or go on for an introduction to a more remote past. Here we suggest taking a taxi. Chiba Prefecture was once mainly farms, supplying flowers and vegetables to Tokyo across the bay. In recent years, housing developments send commuters to Tokyo offices instead, and many industries have been located in the area. Slowly, a rich legacy from the past has been uncovered as the excavators unwittingly dig into the remains of Japan's ancient history.

Great efforts are being made to preserve these relics. There is evidence of forty ancient temples and, it is claimed, thousands of tombs. Farmers are not permitted to disturb them, and the local government is undertaking a program to both explore and protect these ancient sites. You may even spot a microbus carrying a group of housewives dressed for field work. They have been specially trained to check the tombs and excavations for possible new discoveries that will shed more light on the past.

New museums have been built to house these discoveries. One is located in the midst of a nature preserve known as the Hill of Fudoki—Fudoki no Oka.[9] You will notice a flat plain with many new houses as you drive along. A mountain was there before the developers arrived to level the ground and create a new town which will eventually count some 600,000 people. And, one supposes, to uncover some of the artifacts that are now displayed in an attractive museum of antiquities. The park also contains an old primary-school building which appears somewhat colonial in design and two old, sparcely furnished farmhouses, all open to the public.

(If you would like to see more of what Japan is discovering of its past, you might consider another day's excursion to Kokuritsu Rekishi Minzoku Hakubutsu-kan[10] in Sakura, a nearby town where Lord Sakura had his castle. In time it will be Japan's leading research institute in antiquities. And in time, we are told, there will be English-language explanations, but much of the display can be experienced without language since many of the exhibits are designed to give Japanese youngsters a sense of their history. One of the most interesting items is a miniature replica of a Nara-period village. The museum is easy to find. Ask for directions at the train

9. Fudoki no Oka, 978 Sakae-machi Ryukaku-ji, Imba-gun, Chiba-ken; 0476–95–3126
   風土記の丘　千葉県印旛郡栄町竜角寺 978
10. Kokuritsu Rekishi Minzoku Hakubutsu-kan, 117 Jonai-cho, Sakura-shi, Chiba-ken, tel; 0434–86–0123
   国立歴史民俗博物館　千葉県佐倉市城内町117

station as you turn in your ticket and you will be pointed to a window. Look out the window and you will see the museum on a distant hill. A map on the wall shows you how to get there, about a twenty-minute walk. The grounds are impressive, a good place for strolling or a picnic.)

But back to our itinerary. As you leave Fudoki no Oka, watch for Imbanuma (印旛沼), a marshy area popular with fishermen. For some, their outing ended in tragedy. There are many legends of old people who slipped on the muddy embankment and drowned in the swampy waters. Even today, people report seeing their ghosts hovering over the waters that claimed their lives.

There are other destinations. You read earlier in this chapter that the airport is located on what was once imperial pasture lands. Still, the memory lingers on, and you can share it, at the Memorial Park of the Shimofusa Imperial Pasture Grounds.[11] Here you will find the relocated imperial guest house, its roof layered with strips of cypress, its front traditional Japanese, its back—or perhaps it was reversed in the old days—oriented toward the west. A museum houses memories of the past. You can see pictures of the emperorvis iting his pasturelands, the imperial coach that he used, and other mementos of the days when this was a meadow, and the emperor's guests were entertained in an elegant, but traditional, farmhouse.

For those who like flowers in season, Chiba Prefecture's Botanical Gardens[12] are close by. Here dedicated flower raisers come to improve their skills. Paths lead visitors past mounds of blossoms—whatever is in season—and into the less spectacular but gentle elegance of a Japanese garden. The gardens are a source of income for the prefecture. Plants at the peak of perfection are

11. Goryo Boku-jo Kinen-kan, 1–34 Goryo Boku-jo, Sanrizuka, Narita-shi; 0476–35–0442
    御料牧場記念館　成田市三里塚御料牧場 1-34
12. Hana Ueki Center, 80–1 Dojo, Tenjinmine, Narita-shi; 0476–32–0237
    花・植木センター　成田市天神峰道場 80-1

rented to Tokyo offices and restaurants, where they are rotated by the season.

There is another possible destination, a bit difficult to reach, little known to resident or visitor, an excursion that will lead you through the countryside to a temple that time forgot.

Shibayama Nioson Temple (芝山仁王尊). Suddenly you see it, high on a hill, steep, moss-covered steps leading through the massive entrance gate with its elaborate carvings. "Venerable" is the word you will likely choose for this ancient temple, sheltered by towering trees, the eternal quiet broken only by the gentle splash of water, the whisper of the trees.

Once, a visit to Nioson was believed to assure business success, and merchants came all the way from Edo with their petitions. And the gods obliged, attracting more visitors. Then it was one of the busiest and most prosperous temples in all of Japan.

"But for fate," the local priest reports, "we would be just as famous today as Narita-san. It was here, to Nioson, where the pilgrims came in the old days. They didn't mind walking then, all the way from the capital. Now the trains and buses center on Narita City. We are forgotten."

Within the temple grounds is what you have come to see, a museum of antiquities,[13] figures salvaged from the earth that hint of a history yet unexplored. Most appealing are the terra-cotta *haniwa* statues that served to honor the graves of ancient rulers. At first glance they seem so simple, yet they encompass a wide range of humor and emotion in their posture and facial expressions. Few modern sculptors could capture such complexities in so simple a form.

For a moment, in this venerable spot, you may find yourself transported back to Japan's "age of the gods" and sense the

13. Haniwa Hakubutsu-kan, 298 Shibayama, Shibayama-cho, Sambu-gun, Chiba-ken; 04797-7-0004
はにわ博物館　千葉県山武郡芝山町芝山 298

traditions that provide the strength and continuity of modern Japan.

Here our tour ends. You can return to Tokyo (or to the airport, if you are a traveler) well satisfied, knowing that in a few hours you have gained a wide perspective on Japan's history and culture and have seen the beauty of the countryside, in some ways quite unchanged from the days when that history was being made, when the culture was developing.

Or, you may want to continue your Japanese experience. You can book a room at one of the Japanese inns that line the street in front of the temple. And you can be sure that even though you are near the international gateway to Japan, you are still a long, long way from the standard tourist itinerary.

Afterword

MANY PEOPLE, wittingly or otherwise, have helped with the preparation of this book, and I would like to thank them all, the greatest share going to those living in Shitamachi who always had time to talk about the past and share their memories ... and if they didn't know the answers to my questions they would find someone who did. There was the Narita taxi driver who appointed himself my guide—and then turned off the meter; a woman at a shrine who directed me along the route of a mini-pilgrimage; and countless friends and strangers who shared their own special places when they learned I was writing about Shitamachi. I am especially grateful to Meredith Weatherby, who resisted the lures of semi-retirement to return to his office and edit my book, and to Donald Richie, who wrote the foreword. He should have written his own book on old Tokyo and once intended to. A few favorite sentences in my manuscript were taken from the book he never published. I was happy to share them as he shared his knowledge with me. Parts of Richie's foreword and of my chapter on Narita first appeared in *Winds* magazine; I am glad that they can be printed once again in this more permanent form.

To avoid possible confusion: since illustrating the first *Footloose in Tokyo,* Joy Harrison has changed her name to Joana Joy. But her ink sketches, under whatever name, are as charming as ever.

Area-by-Area Finding List

The "weathermark" identifies this book as a production of John Weatherhill, Inc., publishers of fine books on Asia and the Pacific. Editorial supervision, book design, and typography by Meredith Weatherby and Miriam F. Yamaguchi. Production supervision by Yutaka Shimoji. Maps by Shinji Moriyama. Composition by Korea Textbook Company, Seoul. Platemaking and printing, in offset, by Kinmei Printing Company, Tokyo. Bound at the Okamoto Binderies, Tokyo. The typeface of the main text is Monotype Times New Roman, with display in Univers Light.

ABOUT THE AUTHOR

JEAN PEARCE, a free-lance American journalist, has lived in Japan for more than twenty years. Her candid observations on the Japanese scene have appeared in newspapers and magazines both in Japan and overseas. In "Getting Things Done," a widely read and often quoted column in the *Japan Times*, Japan's leading English-language newspaper, she answers an amazing variety of questions from readers with both wit and wisdom. She has written a number of books, published in both English and Japanese, among them *Foot-loose in Tokyo*, an imaginative guide to Tokyo's past and present by way of the Yamanote commuter train line. As a guest lecturer at the University of Maryland's Far East Division, she teaches a course entitled "Japan, a Paradox That Works."

To these many qualifications she now adds yet another in the form of this lively new book, *More Foot-loose in Tokyo.*

The author has had assistance from two able collaborators in gathering together and helping interpret the myriad bits of information that have gone into the book. FUMIO ARIGA is a writer and poet with an amazing store of knowledge about Tokyo, its people, history, and lore. MAKIKO YAMAMOTO, interpreter and translator, was for many years with the American embassy in Tokyo and now serves as a Lady-in-Waiting of the Imperial Household Agency; she is also an accomplished calligrapher, as may be seen from the characters that decorate each chapter opening.